THE
WEALTHY
TRADIE

*How To Make YOUR Business Rake in
The Cash Without Working Like A Dog*

Hugh Bowman

*"WEALTH IS NOT JUST
MONEY; IT'S ABOUT TIME,
RELATIONSHIPS, FAMILY,
AND HEALTH."*

- HUGH BOWMAN

The Wealthy Tradie Book Two- 1st edition
ISBN: 978-0-646-70179-0

ABOUT THE AUTHOR - HUGH BOWMAN

Hugh has a vision, and that is to be the trusted and recognised "go to guy" in Western Regional Victoria for tradie business owners keen to build a strong business, grow their personal wealth and have a great time doing it.

Hugh spent most of his life in small business starting from a family farm and moving on to an industrial refrigeration contracting business post university. During this time he worked closely with many trades from farm hands to plumbers, builders, electricians and many more. Hugh developed a keen sense of what tradies were about and how best to communicate effectively.

A significant career point involved directing and being part owner of a successful and profitable engineering software business focussed on reducing energy consumption in large chilled water plants across Australia, Asia, and Europe.

With an expanding famuily, the local market came calling and Hugh realised he could share his business skills with other business owners in the area. ActionCOACH Geelong was born in 2011.

While he was initially involved in supporting a broad range of businesses during the early years of ActionCOACH Geelong, Hugh has more recently found high levels of success in the trade and technical industries.

His passion and drive for assisting businesses in these areas connects strongly not only with his own key personal interests and professional background but most importantly, it serves his desire to see growth for individual business owners in the trades industries

Outside work Hugh enjoys a wide range of outdoor activities! He keeps fit and active by training for cycling and running events and also enjoys skiing, camping, fishing, and hunting with his 5 boys.

CONTACT:
Hugh Bowman
Ph: 0409 402 474
Email: hugh@actioncoachgeelong.com.au

www.wealthytradie.com.au
www.actioncoachgeelong.com.au

CONTENTS

INTRODUCTION

In many cases you have got this book because you have read my first book The Wealthy Tradie where I go through personal wealth building using your business.

In this book I go through business building strategies that help you make the money to build your personal wealth. It's a book about building and running your business profitably so you can handle the fires, deal with staff, get great paying clients and and make plenty of money.

This is distinctly different from understanding how much money your business needs to generate to build your personal wealth and have fun along the way. All of this is in The Wealthy Tradie Book One. Business strategies to help you make the money is a great start but I do recommend you read both books because the biggest issue you are most certainly facing is:

Your Business Is Running You

I'd say your trades business has probably taken over your life, you've got no time to scratch your backside, let alone check your Profit sheet, and, if you were honest with yourself, you'd probably agree that you're not running your business...

your business is running you!

You're tired. You're frustrated. You're probably not even sure if you're making enough money for all the effort.

Most tradie business owners are what I call "Accidental Owners". You figured you could do a way better job than your old boss or he's driving you mad so you went out and started working for yourself.

Or you were great on the tools and figured becoming the owner was the next logical step. Or your boss simply handed you the keys and said, "Mate, you run it." (This happens more often than you think).

Where is the "running a great business" master class? Most guys I deal with are not stupid or crazy but fail to focus on the business areas that need the most attention. They simply don't know, half know or lacking in confidence to move their business to a more profitable, organised space.

The object of this book is to nail the all too common areas of business that I see most tradies struggle with after having coached hundreds of tradies over the past 11 years.

Why I Work With Tradies?

After working with countless small business owners, it became apparent to me that I really enjoyed working one-on-one with tradies. I generated the best results with these types of owners and the somewhat obvious realisation kicked in; I had spent most of my life working with trades! It explained why we "got" each other and how I was able to understand their businesses in a way many other coaches just couldn't.

I knew the 'lingo' because I lived it – in my engineering days I worked with heaps of different trades to get a job done and so I knew their world... I also knew their pain because I'd personally seen and experienced it too.

So, I made the pivot and said, "That's it, I'm working exclusively with tradies!" back in 2017. And we've hit the ground running ever since. It's been a privilege to see my tradie owners work directly 'on' their business, see their mindset shift to one of a business owner (instead of just an operator) and – best of all – see their revenue grow on average of 50% a year!

Chapter One

How To Turn Your Business Into YOUR Wealth Generator!

Imagine if your business paid for your dream lifestyle… literally all of it… and not just for today, but even when you "put down the tools" for absolute good and retire.

Imagine NOT being flat out or on the go all of the time instead being level-headed, clear and respected because you know you've got all of the time, money and resources behind you to take confident action in your business that
benefits everyone.

And finally, imagine customers literally knocking on your door and leaving raving reviews about what it was like to work with your company, celebrating with a team who loves working for you, and coming home to a family who feels taken care of and grateful to have you in their life. How good would that feel?

See, the thing is: this is entirely possible for you! And every tradie owner out there. We've just been fed a lie that we need to bust our guts to get work, keep work and earn a decent living. But this is a myth. Working around the clock leads to exhaustion and frustration… not real wealth. And real wealth is not just about the dollars – sure, money absolutely plays a role; but real wealth is also about having time, energy, optimal health and great relationships.

Be honest, as it currently stands, is your business currently generating REAL wealth for you?
If not, then we need to make some changes beginning right now.

Now, let's get one thing clear; performing a trade and owning a business is not the same thing! As the owner you are exactly that: the owner. Not the operator. So you need to park the hands-on trades stuff for a moment and focus on business.

Because here's the trick; your business is your key to real wealth. Unlike an employee who MUST hand over their time and effort in order to get paid, a business owner is in a magnificent position where we don't have to do this if we know how to run our business correctly and effectively.
We pay someone else to do the labour, which gives us our time and energy back, and – provided we're

earning a profit in the process (which we should ALWAYS be!) – we get paid for someone doing the hard work for us.

Best of all, when we play our cards right, we can purposely design the business to spit out enough cash for us to live our dream lifestyle. And because nobody's dream lifestyle involves being sick, broke, exhausted, criticised or lonely, this means you'll be on the home run to real wealth! Very nice indeed. So what do we need to do in your business to turn it into your Wealth Generator instead of your pain in the arse?

Read these next few chapters and you'll know exactly what to do!

What is about to follow is a rule book to win in business!

Here we take ACTION in your trades business to improve its profitability, performance and – best of all – get the damn thing funding your dream lifestyle and making sure you become (and stay!) a Wealthy Tradie… even in retirement!

In terms of my proven system to build wealth through your trades business, this is where you currently sit:

In this section we are going to lift your Business Game (significantly!) and dive deep on:

1. The proven strategies & "business hacks" to get your time back.
2. How to control cashflow and navigate the finance stuff so your BUSINESS funds your personal wealth... both today and in retirement!
3. What action to take (and prioritise) in your trades business... starting now.

This business section is split into 2 critical sections:

1. THE FOUNDATIONS

Here we get you out of chaos and back into control! As no great home ever stays standing if it's built on shaky foundations, the same is true for your business. We'll be ticking off the four key pillars that serve as the backbone to building a business that truly supports you, your vision and your needs. These four pillars are:

- **Destination** – In a nutshell: Where the heck are you taking this thing? If you don't know where you're going, it's pretty hard to map out a direct route to get there. So, this pillar encompasses your Business Vision, Business Goals and, the crucial (but often overlooked!) step, which is Business Mindset.

- **Time** – Let's get you your time back by learning how to PROPERLY manage it! In this section you will get tradie-proof tips and techniques to boost your time management so you're working smarter, not harder!

- **Financials** – If you can't build a great business on shaky foundations, you sure as heck can't turn your business into your own personal wealth machine if its financials are kaput!

  Financials is the language of business so if you don't know how to speak this language fluently, you're going to be confused almost all of the time... and quite possibly broke. Rest assured, by the end of this section you'll know exactly how to navigate the financials and "dollars and cents" side of your business!

- **Service Delivery** – You're already great on the tools, so you don't need me to tell you how to do your job. 'Service Delivery' in this context means how you are RUNNING your business, which includes things like: workflow process, managing staff and ensuring your business is optimised to run as smoothly and efficiently as possible.

2. THE BUILDING

Here we get you focused on building the business and making the money! This can only happen after you've laid the CORRECT foundations. (Anyone who tells you otherwise is trying to sell you something!) From there we hone in on:

- **Dream Customer** – Wouldn't it be great if you only ever dealt with customers who you really enjoyed working with? And how good would it be if these same amazing customers actually LOVED doing business with you?! Good news. There's a way to "hack the system" so your dream customers literally come looking for YOU (and you get way more work from the customers you ALREADY have). This chapter is that hack. You're welcome.

- **Marketing** – Have no idea how to get people interested in working with you? Learn how to promote your business with the best marketing techniques and tactics for tradie owners! These marketing tips are SPECIFIC for tradie owners, and after my last 11+ years' working directly with business owners, I know these WILL move the needle on your marketing front (and won't cost you and arm and a leg either!).

- **Sales** – It should go without saying that selling your service is vital if you want to stay in business over the long term. And no, you DON'T have to be slimy or sleezy to get people saying 'yes' to working with you! This section is all about mastering the Sales side of your business without coming across as a douchebag or desperate.

- **Profitability** – The key to turn your business into your personal wealth machine is to make sure the darn thing creates a profit! Too many tradie owners I've worked with have no real clue 'where all their money's going'… and a lot of this has to do with having lousy profit margins in place! In this section, we're going to get clear on Pricing, Productivity, Billing Rules and – the one that trips a lot of you up – getting super clear on what the Real Cost of Labour is!

Chapter Two

THE FOUNDATIONS
From Chaos To Control!

Just like you need to lay down a slab before you build a house, the same is true for your business. Think about it like this: without proper foundations in place, your house would quickly sink into the ground, and you'd end up with cracks and damage all over the place. Now imagine if a storm comes through – Gah! Your home would be cactus! (Wouldn't feel too safe if that property was meant to be keeping you and your family safe, right?!)

So, no way would you build a business on poor foundations! You first need to address the basics – make sure the stumps are deep enough or the slab is level — before you start building a flash property on top, right? You start with the foundations and then you build. In that order.

This rule applies across the board — a decent tiler would never tile directly on a crappy, uneven wall.

A plumber wouldn't install a new bath without first making sure the bathroom floor is sealed. A painter wouldn't slap a coat of paint on a falling down house and call the job done. If you cut corners, it always comes out somewhere.

And nowhere is this more true than when it comes to laying the groundwork in your trades business! Too many tradies come in to see me, wondering why they're stretched and working around the clock — many of these same guys have no clue 'where all the money is' for all this effort. The issue ALWAYS comes down to how they have laid (or not laid) their business foundations. To have any form of success in business, please understand that you MUST move out of chaos and back into the driver's seat of control. You only ever achieve this through mastering the key pillars that hold your whole business up.

I call these foundational pillars 'Stumps'. Because just like stumps, they support the entire load!

Before you spend money and effort on the "exterior" stuff in your business, you must first make sure your stumps are strong, correctly set, level, and able to stand the test of time.

In business, there are four "stumps" that make up the solid foundation to build from.

The Four Foundational "Stumps":

1. **Destination**
2. **Time**
3. **Financials**
4. **Service Delivery**

Now, I have a critical piece of advice for you; you need ALL four for a successful trades business!

Here's a quick way to imagine why all four are needed:
Think of a stool. It has four legs, right? Well, let's say you forget to put a leg on... what happens?
... it topples over!

The stumps are just like that. Miss one and your business falls over and lands right into chaos. Find out one's rotting and halfway to buggery, and guess what? You're working all the time with nothing to show for it and/or the wheels feel like their falling off around you... because — yep, you guessed it.
— your business is actually toppling over under the weight of all the pressure! Time to check what's going on underneath with the foundations.

Because here's the key message: if your stumps aren't set right, your floor will never be level.

In business not only is it vitally important to lay the proper ground work BEFORE you add all the 'bells and whistles' on top (like the great marketing, the effortless sales process and the loyal, hard-working team), but also you need to check in on the foundations regularly… ESPECIALLY (and this is important!) when you make any changes to your business.

The best way to imagine this is to think of a renovation or an extension on a property — before you even pick up the tools, the first thing you'd do is check that the stumps underneath the joint can actually take the new load. You'd ask, "Do we need to reinforce anywhere first?" and you'd act according to what you found underneath the house, right? Ditto with your business mate.

Get familiar with the four key fundamentals because they are what will MOST affect the success (or not) of your business — Destination, Time, Financials and Service Delivery.

I'm going to run through all four in this next section so pay attention.

Chapter Three

Stump #1: DESTINATION

Where the heck are you taking your business? Don't know? Haven't given it much thought? Too busy in the weeds of the day-to-day?

If I could pass on one tiny bit of advice for you, it would be this: *If you don't know where you're going, it's pretty hard to map out a direct route to get there!*

If you don't know where you're going, rest assured, you will still end up somewhere. That's just the way life works. We all must end up somewhere. The only probability with NOT having a final destination in mind (or even a map to follow) is this: *Where you'll end up is probably exactly where you are now.*

Time will have passed, that's all. It might be twenty years "down the road" from now, but a lot will have stayed the same for you and your business. You will probably just live the same year, only twenty times in a row.

Again, that's just the way life works. It keeps chugging on. Unless you have an idea of something different, or you go out and create change for yourself in the only moment you can (Now), you're at the mercy of whatever life throws at you.

Having an idea of where you want to take your business will not only allow you to create a vision of what you want your future to look like, which then enables you to create a map to get there as quickly and effectively as possible... but also, it will ensure you're heading in the direction of somewhere better than where you are currently.

That's why *destination* is one of our Four "Stumps" — one of our four foundational pillars you need to build a successful business!

Destination consists of three parts:

- **Business Vision**
- **Business Goals**
- **Business Mindset**

BUSINESS VISION

A business vision is where it all starts. It not only provides you with a sense of purpose and direction, it also helps guide all your business decisions from here on in — everything from the goals you set, how you show up and lead your team and knowing what actions to prioritise first.

Before you freak out that you need a high and mighty "shoot-for-the-stars" vision, you don't. Of course, you can if you want to – and you should absolutely set stretch targets for yourself – but when it comes to your trades business, your big vision might just be to 'have two teams running'.

In fact, this is something I hear from a lot from the tradie owners I work with — a lot of them want to grow their business but still keep it at a size that's manageable and not more of a headache than it's worth. For example, they want two tradespeople at one site and maybe a team of three working at another site so they can have two jobs running at the same time. Simple.

Maybe you're the same – your business vision might be to own a stress-free business that's easy to run. You might want to own your own workshop, your own gear, and know that the money that's coming in is actually earning you a REAL profit – it's not just money that's barely chipping away at the debt on your vehicles or getting soaked back up in business expenses.

Your vision might simply be to get out of bed knowing that you're doing what you love because you WANT to do it, not because you have to.
Your vision might be to build your business in a sustainable way that allows you to quit the tools whenever you want to so you're not forced to keep working even though your back's stuffed and every inch of your body has had enough you want choice before you desperately need it.

Your vision might be to have a manager that runs the entire show or you might just want a bit of help so you're not responsible for absolutely everything. You might want to earn a squillion bucks, or you might want to earn the exact amount that takes care of your dream lifestyle so you can get on the job with living.

Whatever your vision, get clear on it. We need to know what your "end goal" is (or thereabouts) so we know what we must do in your business and in what order, so we can turn this vision into something you're seeing in real life.

ACTION ITEM

Business Vision

Write down your Business Vision right now.
Please include as much detail as you can.

READ ON....

BUSINESS GOALS

Having worked with many tradie owners and their goals, I know firsthand that many of you can rattle off a few business goals at the top of your head – you don't need much prompting!

The good news is now is the time for you to write down these business goals. Remember that it's critical you set your personal goals first (yes, you must do this) so you have an idea of what to prioritise. (*See my first book for a complete guide on creating personal goals*)

Before you get stuck into it, I have an important note. Make sure these goals are a stretch for you. If you can reasonably expect to achieve the goal right now or you are going to achieve it anyway, it's not a stretch! If you are not stretching yourself, you are not learning or growing or doing anything any better than you are now.

If you don't have a clue how to achieve your goal, then this is even better. Why? You will be forced to learn and to do things differently than what you are currently doing. This will mean you and your business will grow. And what happens when you grow? You get you RESULTS. So stretch yourself!

You'll see some examples on the following page, but here's a few common business goals I often see from tradie owners:

- $X Profit in the next 12 months
- Increase revenue from $X/month to $Y/month in the next two years
- Employ a fully qualified tradesman and an apprentice to have a team of six in the next six months
- Buy a workshop and move in within two years
- Employ an estimator/scheduler so that I don't need to work at night time
- Implement a job management system so that it's easier to manage several teams and therefore the admin person can schedule work and invoice customers before November.

In case you forgot, here's the **S.M.A.R.T** principle again, this time for business goals:

SPECIFIC – Be clear with the goal. Include expectations and avoid generalities.
Example: Buy a workshop/factory in Newtown by October this year.

MEASURABLE – Make sure you can TRACK the progress of the goal. Include things like timelines, costs, quantity and quality
Example: Work on the tools only 3 days per week by June 2022.

ATTAINABLE – Make sure you can actually achieve your goal. You want it to be actionable so that it is in your control.
Example: Delegate the training of new apprentices to my senior guy (make sure I give him the "how-to manual" of how I like it done on Monday.)

RELEVANT – Avoid overwhelming and unnecessary stress by making the goal realistic and relevant to you.
Example: Delegate the training of new apprentices to my senior guy so that I don't have to do it and can instead focus MY time on more dollar-producing activities of the business and/or taking the caravan around Australia (much more fun)!

TIME-BASED – Put a date to complete the goal. Stay focused. Use it to inspire you. Work towards it.
Example: Hire an admin staff to take over all office duties (calls, enquiries, CRM management, orders) by 31st September 2022 so that I no longer have to.

ACTION ITEM

Set Your Business Goals

- Write down the business goals you want to tackle using the SMART method

- Check out the examples list on the following page if you need some more help brainstorming some suitable goals.

READ ON....

Example Business Goals

These are just a guide only – you need to add more personal details to them. Remember to turn your own goals into S.M.A.R.T goals – Specific, Measurable, Achievable, Relevance, Timelines – you must include a date with them.

You usually need 1 or 2 big profit, revenue, business value or time related goals, then a few smaller goals like these:
- Stop operating in credit (overdrafts, etc)
- Increase time between completing and invoicing
- Increase invoice out time
- Use more available services
- Have more technology + systems in the business
- Come up with target for billable hours per tech
- Get better clients
- Increase profitability
- Increase revenue
- Increase business value
- Setup automated sales
- Industrial to Solar. Business acquisition
- Increase my overall revenue (have a specific revenue goal)
- Hire an admin person

- Buy a workshop/factory
- Renovate workshop/factory
- Increase my prices
- Get my weekends back!
- Get quoting up to scratch
- Implement financial report system
- Employ a job manager
- Get an apprentice on
- Get someone else to train the apprentice
- Reduce working hours to 3 days per week by end of year
- Buy an excavator/truck/ute
- Upgrade my current work vehicle
- Pay myself a wage
- Stop doing paperwork at night
- Get more repeat customers
- Advertise and market my business more
- Get a better deal from suppliers

BUSINESS MINDSET

It's time to get your head screwed on! Cardinal Rule #1: There's a critical different between a business operator (someone who works on the tools) and a business owner (someone who works on the business) and a BIG chunk of where this difference comes from is how you think.

You're not to think link an employee anymore. You must think like an owner.

Be Like Barry

Barry was a client of mine for more than five years. We were going through the process of understanding where he was on a personal level with all his assets, super and the like. And, while he's highly-disciplined and fairly smart, he actually didn't have much super. He was going to need a lot more. He said, "Well, I'll pay 'X' dollars away every week. I will just have to make my business do it. I replied, "That is one of the most beautiful statements I've ever heard!"

It was a simple thing because when you start paying yourself like an employee, you are forced to make your business earn enough to do so. This is just one benefit of thinking like an owner, and making your business work for you.

Ultimately, every business has many opportunities. The more effort you put towards these opportunities, the better the outcome you'll get. This is why The Welathy Tradie Book #1 was all about finding out what you really want, and setting your goals. We will now delve into HOW to put your business to work for you so you can achieve those dreams.

When owning a business, you have to set boundaries for yourself by putting money towards paying off debt, buying toys and personal items, and personal time. If your business is booming, then you should be happy. But many times, I find my clients who have a booming business are actually grumpy and tired! Clearly the business is running them – they're not running the business!

Six Key Points To Get You Thinking Like An Owner, Not Like An Operator

Point 1 – Your business should deliver the time and money to support what you want personally.
Your mission in life is not to support your business alone – you want your business to give YOU more life, and more time to do the things you want to do.

Point 2 – Every business has an opportunity to increase output with the owner's motivation or knowledge and skills Every business gets to a certain level and then tapers off. Where it seems to hover is where the owner gets comfortable.

Often businesses growth plateaus at a certain level and motivation is low. The early chapters of this book showed how to work out what you really want and how to put that into a plan.

Let's put strategies in place to help the business get there! This typically occurs through increased effort, increased learning, or increased focus. This is starkly different for an employee mindset because they can try a lot harder, but it might not make any difference to their personal earnings.

Point 3 – Use your business as your Wealth Generator. Make it spin off cash for lifestyle and personal investments like a workshop or residential property. The best way to do this is to pay yourself a wage similar to what you would employ someone to do the same job. Retained cash in the business can then be used for investing in the business, if there is a high return on investment, or withdrawn for your own uses. With most owners I work with, the lure of reinvesting back into the business is very high, so it requires determination to take money out of their business. Remember what got you into business in the first place.

Point 4 – Choose where to reinvest profits. When it comes to reinvesting profits, always consider the Return On Investment (ROI). That is, think about where you get the highest value for the amount of money you are spending. So, if you are considering reinvesting your profits back into the business, you should only ever spend your money, time and energy on the highest ROI project, an equipment purchase or strategy that will get you the most 'bang for buck'.

Point 5 - Treat your business as an entity. If you use and treat the business bank account like your personal account, you will restrict the business potential. You want to make that 'hamster wheel' run faster, so it spins out cash. The more cash it spins out, the better off you are. You don't want to get caught in a trap where you're reinvesting profits endlessly or feeding it back into the business and no cash can be spun out.

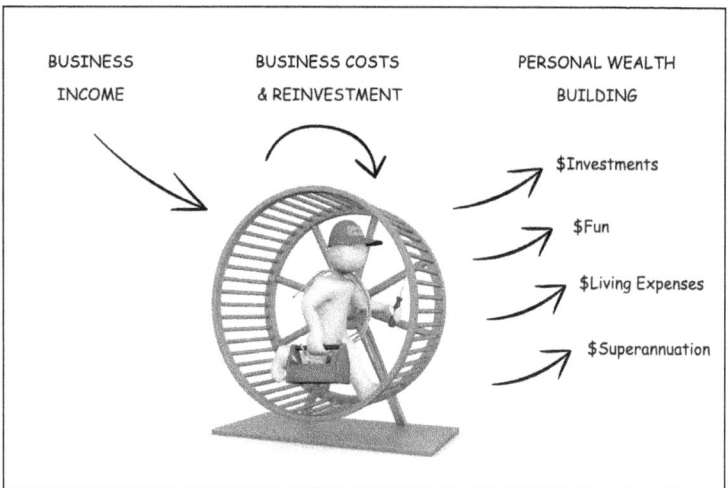

BUSINESS INCOME	BUSINESS COSTS & REINVESTMENT	PERSONAL WEALTH BUILDING
		$Investments
		$Fun
		$Living Expenses
		$Superannuation

If you're a business owner reinvesting the cash profit back into the business, you need to make sure the business value is increasing. I prefer to see equipment financed in the business and the cash taken out for lifestyle and assets outside the business.

If it's a new business, you will need to reinvest it back in; however, at some point you've got to get away from doing that. Here's a fact for you reinvesting cash back into the business does not necessarily make the business worth more. This is a common thought especially with tradies. Some of my younger customers are reinvesting everything back into the business.

They're buying excavators and trucks outright, yet they haven't bought their own house. If you finance the equipment instead, you can use this money to pay down your house so you've got some asset protection outside of the company for example. It's all about tying in those bigger personal goals, thinking about where you get the bigger wins and being smart with what you have and what levers you have at your disposal.

Chapter Four

Stump #2: TIME

If you were a client of mine, and we'd just come out of what's called an 'alignment' meeting together, we would be very clear on "Destination" — that is, the first key "Stump" in building out a solid, sustainable foundation for your business. We would have a few crucial things tucked away as well, but mostly we would be super clear on where exactly you specifically want to take your business and what we might need to prioritise straight away to achieve your goals.

Quick question for you, want to have a guess on the number one thing tradie owners want to fix in their business straight away?

Actually, let me rephrase that, ant to know what issues I almost always fix FIRST?

- Tradie Owners have got no **time** or very little.

- Tradie Owners have got no **money** or they do, they just don't know where the heck it is.

Straight out of that alignment meeting we always work on one of two things, depending on which one is causing the biggest headache at the current moment — and these two things are time or the financials.

Either tradie owners need their time back (they're doing WAY too much), or their financials are a mess. Sometimes, but rarely, they are just ok in both. Meaning they're not drowning in either category but could still make improvements if they thought about it. In all my years as a business coach I have NEVER met a tradie owner who is doing everything absolutely right with time management and nailing the financials of the business.

This is obviously a huge issue as they are two of our **Four Stumps** that serve as the foundation from which we build our business. So please pay attention.

We are starting with "time" here but if financials are your biggest concern right now, you would start there. They are both vitally important for your business, so please read both chapters.

How the hell do you manage your time as a Tradie Business owner? Do you really need to be slogging your guts as much as you are to earn a buck? The short answer is; No mate. You absolutely do NOT!

I'll say this once and say it with the best intentions. You need to work on your time management, and you need to work on it immediately. This isn't an area you can dilly dally around in or keep pushing back until "tomorrow" or "a better time" or "when things die down a bit". What do those things even really mean?

We both know you'll be just as heads-down-bum-up tomorrow if you make no change today. We both know you can't ever get back your time. It's the most precious asset there is so spending it all on work (when you actually DON'T have to!) just doesn't make any sense. You've been thinking about it, you've probably been having a winge about, and you're probably sick and tired of not having any time to yourself anywa. Let's just get in and get it done and if you seriously need more convincing, please realise that literally EVERYONE wins when you master your time management. You, your business, your staff, your family and your mates.

Literally all of them. When I say your business wins, I mean your bottom-dollar results as well. You will literally be better off by not working as much provided and, this is important, you are working on the right things.

Read the strategies below and then act on them. If you need a hand, take me up on a free 90-Minute Strategy Session and we'll tick it off together. Job done. Happy days. (MUCH happier days)!

STRATEGY #1
Work "On" Not Just "In" Business

As the owner not the operator, you must now start working "ON" not just "IN" your business. What does that actually mean? Working IN your business is spending time managing your business as it is today. Working ON your business is spending time on making your business better tomorrow. Every minute you spend working on tasks that can be done by someone else (ie. a JOB) is a minute that you're not planning, strategising and building the best business possible.

Here's the harsh truth. No one else really cares if your business succeeds except you. YOU must therfore be the "Big Picture" guy... NOT the guy stuck in the "weeds" of the business, trying to fix a blocked toilet (either literally or metaphorically).

You're the boss. Your job is to call the shots, delegate jobs, be in charge and make the critical decisions that successfully build your business.

If your business is dependent on YOUR ability to get stuff done, then you are working "IN" your business, not "ON" it. If you're still exclusively on the tools, same deal. It's time to make changes.

When you're working ON the business you are focused on the business not the job. You're working on the important stuff that really makes a difference. Things like improving workflow, increasing profit, finding and keeping better clients, attracting the best workers and so on.

Example jobs of working ON the business:
- Negotiating with suppliers
- Profit increasing strategies
- Systems to increase productivity and job profitability
- Reviewing prices and cost of labour per unit
- Working with a coach to delegate some of your role to staff
- Maintaining relationships with key customers
- Finding & quoting higher paying jobs

STRATEGY #2
Set Maximum Billable Hours

Like I've said before, so many tradie owners are accidental business owners. They first got into their trade to earn some cash, probably worked for a boss for a bit, thought they could do a better job than the boss and make more cash while they were at it, and now they're in business. They never went to business school and probably went from employee to boss in one fell swoop!

This means a lot of tradies like yourself are used to spending time on the tools. Many of you probably prefer it and almost all of you are drawn to it because it's so much easier for you to do than the boring admin work.

This is all well and good, but we need to set some limits around this because as the owner you can't just work on the tools. You have to invoice, make the sale, do the quote, organise the materials, find the work, pay someone else to do a specific job and make sure you've actually got people paying you to do the work. It can get exhausting pretty quick.

Its imperitive to set a limit for billable hours. 'Billable hours' is the amount of time you spend working on the projects that customers actually PAY you for – this is usually the trade itself. I get the work is the "meat and potatoes" of business, and you have to do the job to get the invoice paid. There is a different between a job that needs to be done, and a job that needs to be done by YOU. This is where your tradies come in.

So, you need to set yourself a MAXIMUM LIMIT on how many billable hours you will work each week. This number varies from business to business and might also vary from week to week, depending on some jobs – for example, if you're a maintenance plumber you have to deal with emergency work, so you need to be flexible. This will be your guide though – and you must stick to it, or as close to it as you can, each and every week!

Below you will see an example – this is just a very basic 'rule of thumb' to use as a starting point. It is up to you to set a billable hour target that is realistic and relevant to you. Obviously, if you are still starting out in business, you'll be required to be more "hands on" until you can afford to bring someone else on to absorb the workload. If you have more guys, you're probably spending more time quoting and managing the team, so you're less likely to be personally billing anyway.

It might also be helpful for you to keep in mind Strategy #3 (below), so you're aware of the REAL cost of your time as it may make you reconsider when you chose to bring on new employees (admin and tradies). Example: Max Billable Hours

Size of Business	Max Billable Hours Per Week
1	40
2 - 4	28 – 32
5 - 8	20 – 28
8+	<16

ACTION ITEM

Set Your Billable Hours

- Set your Maximum Billable Hours!

- … Stick to it!

READ ON....

STRATEGY #3
Allocate Dollar Per Hour ($/Hr) To Your Activities

This one will make you see the power of time management in a whole new light! We're going to do a bit of a "time study" and write a list of ALL the things you currently do in business and put a price to it!

Once you do this, you'll see things completely differently — and it will be game changing for you and your business.

We are going to allocate an 'hourly rate' to your activitities. How much it would cost you to pay someone else to do the same job. You will see the real value in where you're spending your time. Wait until you see the hourly rate you are missing out on when you focus on the small stuff.

Fun (or not so fun) Fact. I have my own list and I still have to reread my own rules. Every now and again I'll go out and clean my car after a client meeting to clear my head or find myself mowing the laws out the front only to remind myself, "This is actually costing me way more than I think to do this right now!"

Example: Working Out The REAL Cost Of Your Time!

ACTIVITY Stuff you're doing in your business	$ Hour Rate How much it would cost to PAY someone to do it for you!
Wash the car	$20
Mow the office lawn	$40
Plumbing work	$90
Deliver materials to guys on site	$40
Bookkeeping	$60
Service excavators	$90
Quoting/Sales	$200+
Working ON business	$200+
Learning/Planning Profit Increases	$200+
Negotiating with suppliers	$200+
System to calculate job profitability	$200+
Reviewing Prices	$200+
Maintaining relationships with key customers	$200+

ACTION ITEM

Allocate $/Hr To Every Activity That You Do

Your turn. Think of all the activities you're currently doing for your business – and list the hourly rate next to each one!

READ ON....

STRATEGY #4: The Shit List

We all have stuff we just hate doing in our business. Whatever it is, it just pisses us off. We hate doing it every time we do it and it never gets easier. It's just shit, and we wouldn't do it if we didn't have to. Well, I have a proposal for you, let's NOT do the shit stuff!

I have a thing called the "Shit List". It consists of anything you hate doing, you're not good at doing or anything that takes you ages to do. The rule is: anything on this list, Defer it. Give the job to someone else. This is the beauty of being the boss. Plus, your time is almost always better spent elsewhere. Of course, some things are a necessary evil (like quoting) but most things you can easily handball to someone else.

For example, so many tradie owners hate paperwork, they hate bookkeeping and invoicing. If this is you add it to the Shit List and quickly organise for someone else to do it.

Don't like some aspects of managing staff like doing the training or regular reviews? Pay a HR person to do it. Get them to come in when you need them and organise it all for you.

Sick of cleaning the workshop after the guys come back from the job and just drop their stuff everywhere, leaving dirt and crap all over the place? Allocate the job to someone else. Put a system in and tell the guys, "This week, so-and-so is responsible for making sure my workshop's clean, so-and-so is looking after the trucks and coming to me if there's any problems there, and so-and-so is on kitchen duty."

Even better, tidy your workshop, take a photo & put it on the wall saying: This is how the workshop needs to be left every time you leave it! Set expectations. Allocate jobs. Throw a few extra bucks at something that brings you nothing but pain. Get it on the Shit List and palm it off to someone else.

ACTION ITEM

Come Up With Your Own SHIT List

- Write your own Shit List. Including all jobs you hate doing, are not good at, or that take you ages to do.
- Organise for someone else to do them
- Prioritise getting your Shit List off your plate ASAP so you can focus your attention on better things

READ ON....

STRATEGY #5: Default Diary

Let's now get some control back into your working week! What we're going to do now is set up a "Default Diary". This is an ideal week where we organise your calendar with chunks of time blocked out at specific times to work on non-billable tasks.

This way you're spending specific days (or parts of days) doing just one important business activity – and you do it and the same time, for the same amount of time, each week.

For example, let's say you organise two separate time slots for quoting a week. One on Tuesday afternoon and another on Thursday mornings. How's this useful? Well, your week won't ever again be filled with small little quoting jobs all over the place and you can quickly wrap your head around when you'll be quoting.

Just imagine someone calls you up and says, "Hey I need a quote" You won't have to think twice. You already know what days you quote. You reply "Yeah, I reckon I've got a spot in my diary Tuesday arvo for you…" Suddenly you've got people slotting right into your diary in a way that works for you.

But that's not all. Blocking out times in this way means you're not suddenly switching from one

	MON	TUES	WEDS	THURS	FRI	SAT
6:00AM						
7:00AM	TEAM MEETING					
8:00AM				QUOTING	Work on	
9:00AM					business	
10:00AM						
11:00AM						
12:00PM						
1:00PM						
2:00PM		QUOTING				
3:00PM						
4:00PM						
5:00PM						
6:00PM						

business activity to the next, which requires a lot more effort and energy than you think. There's a lot of brain science behind it. Turns out we are way more productive when we're laser-focused on one specific thing instead of splitting our attention every two seconds.

Make a rule: block out the time to do the task, and then when it comes time to do the task, switch off your phone (divert it to one of the guys if you're worried about customers calling.) This way you have no distractions and are free to work on the stuff that matters.

Ideally, you want a Default Diary that resembles your DREAM week. Obviously, life happens and so we've got to be flexible from time to time. But you want to stick to it as much as humanly possible. Here's another tip: if you do have to be flexible, instead of just thinking, "Ah, well there goes my quoting time that week because now I have to do X,

Y or Z…" Pivot. Switch on your Business Owner Mindset instead. So what if that happened? You'd reschedule that quoting timeslot to another time you are free that week. You still MUST do it. This is the key. At the very least, tradie owners need to block out time for "Quoting " and "Working ON The Business". Ideally, you want to bang a weekly meeting in with your team too.

Have a crack – remember it's YOUR week so you want it to work for you. Don't skip this step – once you get into a rhythm (which'll happen pretty quick) you'll absolutely love how much you can get done and why all of sudden things seem less hectic and way more smooth!

	Monday	Tuesday	Wednesday	Thursday	Friday
7:30	Team meeting		Office	Office	Office
7:45	Vehicle checks		invoicing	invoicing	invoicing
8:00	Office		ordering materials	ordering materials	ordering materials
8:15	invoicing				
8:30	ordering materials	Quoting			
8:45					
9:00					Business
9:15					management
9:30					
9:45	On tools		On tools	On tools	
10:00					Working
10:15					on the
10:30					business
10:45					
11:00					
11:15					
11:30					
11:45					
12:00	LUNCH	LUNCH	LUNCH	LUNCH	LUNCH
12:15	LUNCH	LUNCH	LUNCH	LUNCH	LUNCH
12:30					
12:45					
13:00					
13:15	On tools	On tools	On tools		On tools
13:30				Quoting	
13:45					
14:00					
14:15					
14:30					
14:45					
15:00					
15:15					
15:30					Return calls
15:45					Plan next week
16:00	Return calls	Return calls	Return calls	Return calls	Tidy Up
16:15	Plan next day	Plan next day	Plan next day	Plan next day	Tidy Up
16:30					
16:45					
17:00	family time	family time	family time	family time	family time

ACTION ITEM

Create Your Own Default Diary

- Create your own default diary and put it somewhere so you can see it all the time.

- Start running all your days according to this new schedule ASAP

READ ON....

STRATEGY #6
Recruit an Admin & a Worker

It's time to recruit one admin staff member and a worker. I know what you're thinking, "I can't afford that…" or "How the bloody hell…" Look if you're not there yet, you're not there yet but in a lot of circumstances, this actually isn't the case. Go back to the cost of your hourly activities and see what you might be doing that, quite frankly, is a waste of your time. Sure, the task needs to be done, but it doesn't need to be done by the business owner.

Remember business owners work on big things. That doesn't mean you need to fuel your ego and stop doing all the "small" stuff immediately; it means you've got to focus your time on where the money really is and prioritise this as soon as you can.

If you've got stuff on your Shit List that can also be absorbed by hiring a new team member, even better. This gives you back your sanity but also frees up your time – which you can spend either working ON the business or having a breather.

Keep in mind, you DON'T need to hire support staff or a worker fulltime if you can only afford to get someone on 1 – 2 days a week. Sometimes that's the amount of work you only have available anyway; particularly if you have a smaller sized business.

My client Tim started with an admin staff 1– 2 days/ week and now we are looking at potentially ramping this up so that he can spend more time out of the books and back into billable hours. He makes more money getting paid to be a chippy than he does doing the books, which he can pay someone else to do. It's about becoming smarter with how you spend your time and choosing activities that will give you the best return in exchange for your time, effort, attention and energy.

STRATEGY #7
Set rules around work time

Time to set rules around your work times mate! I know you're the owner, but you can't keep up with the excuse that you 'need' to be working around the clock. It simply is not true. Of course you have got more stuff on your plate than an employee and this sees you pulling longer hours, especially at first. But you still need to come up with some form of "Start and Stop" times. You are not a machine. You're a human being. And you can't keep pressing your foot to the floor and not expect the brake pads to wear down.

At some point you'll have metal on metal and no one wants that. It's time to come up with your own rules around when you're working – and more importantly, when you've clocked off for the day (for good!).

Before I give you some starting points, I just want to tell you I hear this all the time from my tradie owners; "Yeah, but I just get stuck on site. If I've nearly finished the job, I'll just stay and finish it…" Well, mate you have broken your rule! You don't miss the first hour of your footy match, so why do you think it's okay if you just come home an hour or two late? Don't break your own rules! How can anyone possibly take you seriously if you can't even keep your own word to yourself.

I get that you need flexibility and sometimes is it logical to put in an extra half hour so you don't have to make the drive tomorrow. Of course! That's why when we set our rules we make allowances for flexibility. For example, we'll say be home by 5pm two nights each week. Stayed back late twice already? Sorry, can't do it again. What would be the point? You'll get stuck into the bad habit and before you know it, the whole rule book has been thrown out the window. You're a man of your word, so own your rules. Set rules that work for you so that you can keep them.

Example Rules around work time:

- Be home by 5pm, 2 nights each week
- Max 4 hours work on weekend
- NO work at home (or put a limit on it!)

ACTION ITEM

Set Rules Around Your Work Time

Come up with some rules for yourself around when you do and don't work – be realistic, but be firm with yourself.

READ ON....

Chapter Five

Stump #3: FINANCIALS

Did you know that business has a language?!
Yep, it sure does. Like most activities, there's a
'lingo' going on. Ever heard your wife (or your
sister or your friends' partner) talk about shopping
or something and it's like they're actually speaking
another language?! Or what about on MasterChef
where they talk about 'mincing' and 'julienning' and
'braising'? What about at the doctors where they
know all about 'microbiomes' and 'ligaments' and
'adipose tissue'?

They're all completely different languages!
And it seems like those who are the best at their
individual activity speak the language of it fluently!
(While the rest of us can barely understand it.)
Business is the same. It has its own language and if
you can't speak it, then you're kinda stuffed.

Want to have a guess what the language of business is? … Accounting!

Did I just hear crickets and/or someone sprinting off in the distance? Stick with me here mate, because this is important. Accounting is all about recording, analysing and summarising FINANCIAL transactions.

If you don't know how to speak the language of financials, you're kinda up the creek! And if your accountant opens their mouth and starts rattling off names and phrases you've never heard of… it can be bloody overwhelming.

The trouble a lot of tradie owners have is they've never studied accounting. They probably didn't bloody want to, either. But this becomes a very big problem very quickly when you are running your own business. You simply MUST know the finances of your business. There's no 'ifs' or 'buts' about it – understanding where you sit financially is critical.

You cannot bury your head in the sand or not look at it simply because you don't like it or want to do it – that is a quick way to go broke. Too many of my tradie clients just don't know what's going on with the 'dollars and cents' side of their business and this is alarming.

Likewise, too many of them "don't know where the money's going" in their business – they've got plenty of work, their reputation's awesome, they've got guys pulling their weight… but they just can't seem to see the cash in their business… where's it all going?

Listen up because it is possible to go broke making a profit. Yep – mind blowing. But true. Even more so if you're not capturing all your expenses at all, or correctly!

When it comes to Financials, I have **FIVE GOLDEN RULES**, which all business owners need to know and master. These rules are non-negotiable, and I'm about to walk you through each of them in a way that won't hurt your head but will stop you from going broke. Know the rules, follow the rules, set yourself up for Financial success!

The Five Golden Rules of Finances:

RULE #1: Set Up An Accounting System And Use It To Its Full Capacity.

RULE #2: Unlock The Power of Your Profit & Loss Statement!

RULE #3: Don't Stop At Profit & Loss Understand Your "REAL" Financial Performance.

RULE #4: Separate Your Cost of Sales And Know How Much You Need To Break Even!

RULE #5: Master The Cash Gap Strategy! (This Is The Best Way To Get Paid On Time & Chase Up Late Payers)

RULE #1
Set Up An Accounting System And Use It To Its Full Capacity!

Like I mentioned, most tradies I work with don't put enough focus on their financials. I once had a business owner call me who's been in business for seven years.

He said to me, "I don't have any record of my sales and I don't know how much money I make, but I do know I got a $40,000 tax bill." Err. That's a problem.

To give you an idea, at the time it was Covid-19 — so this particular client was also keeping up with JobKeeper payments and, to make matters even more stressful, with all of the lockdowns going on, they hadn't done much business.

They'd been losing money and they knew it. But with no real record of anything, they had no idea how much or what the full story was!

Guys, we MUST have some urgency and seriousness around your numbers! This is what keeps the roof over your head, the tax man away and you in business!

The very FIRST thing you need to do is have an accounting system in place. An accounting system automates your business's financial functions and records all of your accounting needs for you. You can also go in the back end and organise things like accounts payable, accounts receivable and payroll (as well as heaps of other vitally useful stuff!) – it is game changing for your business.

It sounds extremely basic, but it's surprising the number of trades companies I've come across that aren't actually familiar with accounting systems such as Xero or QuickBooks or MYOB. Mark my words: the time of keeping track of stuff with a notepad and pen is over. It is not enough to support you in business, and neither is outsourcing your entire financial responsibility to your accountant.

You must be across your own business numbers. Remember: no one cares as much about the success of your business as you.

By having your own accounting system, you can access important financial documents yourself. You should be checking these documents regularly anyway.

Even a lot of folks who DO have one of these systems in place sadly don't use it to its full potential. As just one example, I once came across a business that used the accounting system Xero but for whatever reason, they just didn't enter their invoices! Don't do this. Enter your invoices. You want your system to be capturing everything. This will keep you, your business, and your clients safe.

Then, get this — another company I dealt with had a bookkeeper who didn't alert the owner that they had been UNPROFITABLE FOR 12 MONTHS, and before you think it – no, this is not the bookkeeper's fault. You would however hope your bookkeeper would flag something like that with you.

Here's the bottom line: it's the owner's job to know how the business is going. If the bookkeeper missed something, then it falls back on the owner that they weren't adequately trained on his processes and how to use the accounting system in a manner that best served his business. You must always be clear on expectations.

Pay attention here: the buck always stops with you. It's time to open your eyes to the financial health of your business so this does NOT happen to you where you suddenly wake up and see you've been losing money for an entire year! Knowing your numbers is not rocket science, but it does require (at the bare minimum!) your attention.

If you don't currently have an accounting system, get one. Jump on Google, have a look at the options out there (Xero, QuickBooks or MYOB are good if you need some suggestions) and get the ball rolling. There should be easy tutorial videos on how to use each system – and always speak directly to your accountant if you need more information. No question is a dumb question. The only dumb thing to do is to ignore your financials.

RULE #2:
The Power of Your Profit & Loss Statement

When was the last time you checked your Profit & Loss Statement?

A Profit & Loss Statement (P&L Statement) is a business owners' best mate. It explains all the income and expenses that lead to your company's profits (or losses) over a period of time.

PROFIT & LOSS	
SALES	
Maintenance	$20,000
Contracts	$30,000
	$50,000
COST OF SALES	
Materials	$10,000
Contractors	$3,000
Equipment Hire	$2,000
Wages - site	$15,000
	$30,000
EXPENSES	
Rent	$2,000
Insurance	$1,000
Phone	$1,000
Other	$6,000
	$10,000
PROFIT	**$10,000**

Something that is invaluable information for an owner who is keen to know whether they're making a profit or not. Aside from what we just spoke about in Rule #1, one of the many benefits of using an accounting system is you can generate a current P&L Statement at the click of a button.

A few tradies get into a bad habit of thinking the bookkeeper will "take care of all that", but here's a wise bit of information for you. It's absolutely critical you are across key financial metrics in your business and how they fared over each month.

You want to see the results side by side so you can notice any trends that might be going on so that if there are any issues, you can tell right away and then immediately solve the issue. The financial metrics the P&L Statement include are things like income (from sales/jobs), cost of sales, expenses and both Gross and Net Profit.

Here's just a quick outline of a basic Profit & Loss statement:

Sales/Income: Everyone seems to hate the word sales, but by this, we simply mean work. That is, the amount of money you bought in through your jobs each month. This can also be called "income" –but often you will have "other income" listed in your P&L statement as well like interest on your bank account or money from government training incentives.

Cost of Sales: Cost of Sales includes all the costs required to do the job. That is, things you absolutely can't do the job without like the labour and the materials, etc. All these make up the "cost of the sale". It's helpful to think of these as direct costs of doing business.

Expenses: This is the amount of money going out the door! This includes business costs like rent, phone bills, insurance, accounting fees, etc. Now these are different from "Cost of Sale" items as Expenses are all the overhead costs

Stuff you always have to pay regardless of the specific job. Generally the default P&L Statement in your accounting system will lump all your expenses together, which sometimes includes 'Cost of Sales' items (like materials and labour) but we actually want to tweak this so that any expenses directly related to the job ('Cost of Sale' items) are separated out from our normal business expenses. You can get your accountant to quickly tweak this for you, but don't worry about that just yet, I'll explain it in detail in Rule #4.

Gross Profit: The amount of money you're left with if you take away the Costs of Sales from the Income.

Net Profit: The amount of money you're left with after paying ALL your business expenses.

Let's take look at a real-life example on the following page.

Profit and Loss

	Feb-22	Jan-22	Dec-21	Nov-21	YTD
Income					
Commercial	$17,983	$1,291	$4,536	$0	$27,884
Domestic	$0	$0	$545	$160	$1,882
Industrial	$0	$2,269	$892	$14,202	$31,251
Miscellaneous Income	$0	$0	$0	$0	$20,000
Solar	$29,998	$32,552	$42,673	$46,175	$308,159
Total Income	**$47,981**	**$36,112**	**$48,646**	**$60,538**	**$389,176**
Less Cost of Sales					
Contractor	$0	$0	$823	$0	$823
Electrical Inspection	$1,273	$0	$1,733	$1,918	$10,720
Franchinsing Fee	$874	$874	$1,024	$874	$2,960
Materials	$7,411	$7,493	$5,570	$14,104	$69,647
Site Staff - Superannuation	$1,396	$1,575	$1,224	$1,530	$10,396
Site Staff - Wages	$13,964	$15,751	$12,236	$15,295	$104,246
Total Cost of Sales	**$24,918**	**$25,693**	**$22,609**	**$33,721**	**$198,791**
Gross Profit	**$23,063**	**$10,419**	**$26,036**	**$26,817**	**$190,385**
Plus Other Income					
Interest Income	$0	$0	$0	$0	$0
Training Incentive	$0	$9,169	$0	$2,500	$32,638
Total Other Income	**$0**	**$9,169**	**$0**	**$2,500**	**$32,638**
Less Operating Expenses					
Accounting & Audit Fees	$191	$191	$191	$1,191	$2,527
Advertising	$32	$395	$0	$0	$796
Bank Charges	$42	$22	$260	$21	$602
Bookkeeping	$135	$146	$131	$266	$1,749
Client Gifts	$0	$0	$0	$147	$147
Conference Costs	$0	$0	$337	$0	$337
Consultancy Fees	$1,795	$1,795	$1,795	$1,795	$12,796
Freight Charges	$0	$0	$25	$0	$145
Fuel & Oil	$929	$954	$1,135	$1,265	$8,253
Insurance	$0	$0	$0	-$172	$1,579
Interest Expense	$540	$890	$468	$490	$5,045
Internet Account	$73	$0	$145	$145	$654
Licenses & Registrations	$242	$45	$0	$1,024	$1,425
Long Service Leave	$0	$418	$0	$0	$1,292
Meals	$25	$65	$0	$0	$90
Office Superannuation	$172	$126	$105	$189	$1,739
Office Supplies/Equipment	$247	$1,304	$685	$1,058	$4,120
Office Wages & Salaries	$1,824	$2,446	$1,568	$1,890	$19,423
Plant & Equipmnt less than $1k	$34	$0	$0	$0	$34
Protective Clothing/Equipment	-$213	$0	$427	$131	$415
Rent	$509	$636	$509	$636	$4,164
Rubbish/Tip Fees	$85	$85	$112	$85	$532
Staff Amenities	$85	$179	$805	$346	$1,985
Subscriptions	$70	$52	$52	$294	$909
Telephone	$261	$328	$307	$307	$2,447
Tolls/Parking	$6	$59	$34	$0	$141
Tools > $1000	$278			$439	$1,880
Training		$0	$0	$0	$1,343
Vehicle Registration & Insuran	$0	$61	$0	$0	$4,266
Vehicle Repairs & Maintenance	$159	$12	$624	$26	-$1,305
Workers' Compensation	$0	$0	$0	$358	$420
Total Operating Expenses	**$7,519**	**$10,210**	**$9,715**	**$11,932**	**$79,949**
Net Profit	**$15,543**	**$9,379**	**$16,322**	**$17,385**	**$143,074**

As you can see from the electrical company's Profit & Loss (P&L) Statement, you can see a complete breakdown of where all the income is coming from, as well as the costs associated with actually doing the job.

These Cost of Sale items include stuff like site staff wages, materials, the cost of electrical inspections and any contractor fees involved. In this particular example, you can also see that there is a 'Franchising Fee' that has also been included in the Cost of Sale (COS). This could be listed as an overhead expense as well, but this tradie owner likes including it as part of his actual COS.

You can get your accountant to tweak your Cost of Sale items for you, so what you want appears in this section instead of just being lumped in with all the overhead expenses. That way you can tell exactly what cost is required to do the job, which has many extra benefits for you. I'll explain more on this in Rule #4.

As you can see from the example P & L Statement, when we minus ('less') our Costs of Sale total from our Income total, we get our Gross Profit for the month, as demonstrated.

But Gross Profit is never the full story as we have overhead costs to factor in as well.

Moving through this particular statement, we can also see any 'other income' that's coming into the business outside of the actual sales from the work done. As you can see, we have a section for interest income, but over this particular time period we've only had extra income come into the business via a couple of government training incentives.

Next up, you can see a huge chunk of Expenses. These are the 'operating' costs ie. the overhead costs of the business that AREN'T included as part of the sale. Things like accounting fees, advertising, conference costs, internet, admin costs... *you can read the list.*

To tie it all off, we have a very important number. Our Net Profit where we can actually see how much money we made for each month. As you can see, having our monthly profits available to us side by side lets us quickly see how our profits are performing over time.

In this example, we can see that our profits in Jan 22 were pretty light on – and if we dig under the bonnet there, we can see we actually had extra income of

$9,169 from a government training initiative come in. Why was our profit lower? Well, not only did we do less sales for the month (Covid getting in the way again), which we can literally see on our statement, we can also see that our expenses were slightly up for the month too. We were running some extra advertising (to make up for the Covid slump), which meant we had some direct fees there as well as a few hundred bucks in overtime to the staff member to run the advertising for us. Oh, and we also happened to buy some new office supplies that month too, which we can see listed.

You can actually start to see the story of what happened? So, if that DIDN'T happen, and you can see that a month's profit margin is off, or there's an expense that's skyrocketed or something, you can get to the bottom of it. This is the simple power of a P& L Statement.

RULE #3

Don't Stop At Profit & Loss...
Understand Your "REAL" Financial Performance

Hands up if you do any cash jobs.... or don't have every little thing captured in your accounting system?

Chances are, it's all of us.

Here's the deal: an accounting system like Xero, Quickbooks, or MYOB are great financial recording tools, not financial or business analysis tools. This means if you're not recording stuff in them, you're not going to have all the information you need to properly assess your business and therefore, work out how it's ACTUALLY performing.

The best way to do this to have a spreadsheet working alongside your accounting system. Before you roll your eyes or put this step in the 'too hard' basket, I want to remind you how critically important it is to know your numbers. I do this step myself and I do this for EVERY trades business I coach. It's too important NOT to do. And sure, you'll need all this stuff come tax time anyway, so you'll end up having a super useful document where everything is captured in one place (no need to search up and down and all over the joint to find a gazillion different documents), but that's not the point.

The point is that you MUST start taking an interest in this stuff. If this single step is what gets my guys looking at their financials, then I consider the battle half won. The act of having a separate spreadsheet means you must first look into your accounting system (yep!) to find the numbers that are appropriate for the month, and then put them into the spreadsheet. This is useful for many reasons, which I'll explain in second, but here's the big one: Your accounting system can't help you unless you can put your numbers in a format that actually makes sense! So, let's get the numbers making sense.

Financial Ratios and "REAL" business performance measurements gives business owners a pulse on how their business is doing. I put "real" in quotes because almost every business I look at has things that are actually not in their accounting system, or that are in their accounting system but distort the real performance.

A distortion might be that the owner rents out half their shed to a mate, so the income on their P&L statement is falsely high... or maybe they've got pseudo work items purchased through the business (roof racks for the owner's vehicle that could be used for carrying materials but were really purchased for going camping), which is throwing their expenses out.

Other items that might simply be missed (or misrepresented) could be a TV that should be in the lunchroom for training people, or the home computers, or the partner's car. You get the gist. And then there's the old favourite... undeclared cash.

Before you get all secretive, this step is not about me trying to play the tax man – I'm trying to get an understanding of the REAL financial performance of your business. You need to know what the numbers are really up to. You can't fix what you can't see, so you need to start seeing clearly... even if it's just for your eyes only. Know what your REAL expenses and outgoings are for the business.

To help you understand what's "REAL", the simple question to ask yourself is 'Would I buy that item for an employee?' If you wouldn't do it in reality, then it's probably a pseudo work item, so we want to remove it when we're assessing our financial performance on the separate spreadsheet.

"REAL" Financial Performance
My free tool aptly called 'REAL Financial Performance' is exactly that – a spreadsheet that captures your 'actual' business stats and compares them from month to month (comparison is key!). It will give you the "real" view by allowing room

for cash jobs and whatever else might not be in the books, which will let you see what's really going on in your business without having to make a huge song and dance about it. You'll get the real performance for each month, but also it calculates the averages for you so you can get a ballpark on what you're pulling in most months, and – perhaps most impressively – it will calculate two very important figures for you, which Xero and QuickBooks won't automatically do – the Cost of Sales percentage (COS %) and your Profit Margin percentage (this compares profits to sales and tells you how well your company is doing overall). The COS % alone is vitally important as it will let us hit Rule #4 (explained further below).

This spreadsheet will help you do three things:

1. Actually look at your numbers (and understand them)
2. Get a "REAL" picture of your profit once cash jobs (and other stuff not in the books) are factored in
3. Get two key Financial Stats that will determine your "Break Even".

The financial numbers we're really keen to measure are:

- REAL Sales (Income)
- Gross Profit
- REAL Expenses
- REAL Profit
- Cost of Sales %
- Profit Margin %

My Stats - Business

REAL FINANCIAL PERFORMANCE

FINANCIAL RATIOS

Date	Income (from P/L)	Plus Adjustmts (other income or cash)	SALES (real)	Cost of Sales (from P/L)	Gross Profit	Expenses (from P/L)	Less Adjustments (non business related expenses)	Expenses (Real)	PROFIT (Real)	Cost of Sales % of Sales (COS/Sales)	Profit Margin % (profit/sales)
Nov-21	$ 60,537	$ 2,500	$ 63,037	33,720	$ 29,317	11,932		$ 11,932	$ 17,385	53.5%	27.6%
Dec-21	$ 48,545	$ -	$ 48,645	22,609	$ 26,036	9,714		$ 9,714	$ 16,322	46.5%	33.6%
Jan-22	$ 36,111	$ 9,169	$ 45,280	25,692	$ 19,588	10,210		$ 10,210	$ 9,378	56.7%	20.7%
Feb-22	$ 47,980	$ -	$ 47,980	24,918	$ 23,062	7,518		$ 7,518	$ 15,544	51.9%	32.4%
Mar-22											
Apr-22											
May-22											
Jun-22											
			Ave (FY)		Ave (FY)			Ave (FY)	Ave (FY)		
Averages			$ 51,238		$ 24,501			$ 9,844	$ 14,657	52%	29%

I'll run you through an actual example using our electrician mate, but here's the snapshot of what his REAL Financial Performance spreadsheet looks like:

Don't let all the numbers throw you off, remember we only fill out one month at a time. You would simply open up your own Profit & Loss (P&L) Statement, get the number you need and enter it in the correct spot ('cell') in the REAL Financial Performance spreadsheet. It's actually much simpler than first appearances suggest – the greyed-out boxes are automatically calculated for you, so you don't need to do any work there.

Let's break down each column:

- **Income:** Use the same number on your P&L Statement
- **'Plus Adjustments':** Add in any other income that's NOT being captured in your accounting system (this is where those cash jobs go!)
- **Sales** (REAL): This is your REAL income figure – it will automatically work it out for you.
- **Cost of Sales**: Use the same number on your P&L Statement. (You will need to ask your bookkeeper or your business coach to reclassify 'Materials & Labour as direct costs as opposed to expenses.) See Rule #4 for more info.
- **Gross Profit:** This is your REAL gross profit - it will automatically work it out for you.
- **Expenses:** Simply use the same number on your P&L Statement
- **Less Adjustments:** Add in any other NON BUSINESS related expenses here (like the work lunchroom TV that ended up in your loungeroom)
- **Expense** (REAL): This is your REAL expenses – it will automatically work it out for you.
- **PROFIT** (REAL): This is your REAL profit (VERY important!) – it will automatically work it out for you.
- **Cost of Sales %:** This is the total costs to do the work for the month – it will automatically work it out for you.
- **Profit Margin %:** This is the measure of how profitable you were for the month – it will automatically work it out for you.

Using our electrical company as an example, if we put their P&L Statement and their REAL Financial Performance measurement side by side, this is what we get. (See sperate pages 86 & 87.)

Can you see where we have pulled each number from?

On their P&L statement, we can see that their income for Feb 2022 was $47,981 – so we put this same number into our REAL Financial Performance spreadsheet under the 'income' column. We move along the spreadsheet in this same way – wherever it says "From P/L" it always means it's the exact same number highlighted on the Profit & Loss Statement.

These columns include: Income, Cost of Sales and Expenses. The columns we're really interested in and that you need to add something different to are the "Plus Adjustments" (other income or cash) and "Less Adjustments" (non business related expenses).

For this electrical business, we can see that in Feb we didn't have any cash jobs or extra income ("Plus Adjustments), nor any expenses that were put through the books but weren't actually for the business ("Less Adjustments"). That said, you can see in January 2022 we did a couple of cash jobs to a total of $9,169 and so we always put that in when necessary.

Now, because we have four consecutive months of REAL financial data for the business, we can start to get an idea of the overall financial story – they average $51,236 in sales (work) a month with an average of $14,657 in profit. That's REAL profit.

Remember this number because it's going to be really interesting when we get to Rule #4 and we work out their "Break Even Number"... you'll find out that this is actually NOT enough for them to break even in their business, so they are actually LOSING money!! (Ouch). This is why just one of our 'Financial Ratios'– Cost of Sales % – is so important because it lets us determine how much we really need to be earning in profit to make a return on investment.

You can see here that the average Cost of Sales in Feb was 51.9%, with a total average of 52%. This means that about half of our total income is spent on doing the job itself (like paying for materials and labour).

While every business is different, an average COS is normally 55 – 70% of sales. Because trades businesses are quite labour-heavy, they tend to be on the higher end, but it's always a good idea to work out the Cost of Sales in your own business and look at ways to minimise it where possible (this might mean looking at pricing changes, calculating the

REAL cost of labour, etc).

Finally, for this particular electrical company, we can see that our Profit Margin for February was 32.4% with an average of 29%.

Plus, we've also got a couple of cool charts that allow us to see our Sales and Profit trend over time. Just a heads up: when you're a business owner, "the trend is your friend". A trend allows you to gauge what the heck your business is doing and what direction you're really heading in (up or down! Better or worse...)

SALES (real)

PROFIT (Real)

This is just one reason why comparing your monthly performance over time is so important. Even if you just have four months of comparative data like we do here, you can start to see the business trend – so imagine what the charts would show if we had 6, 12, 18 months of business history.

The numbers will actually have MEANING instead of just being a bunch of random numbers thrown at you! And you won't ever need to stare at your accountant with a blank face ever again – because you'll know how to quickly and easily understand the numbers yourself. There's nothing quite like feeling like an owner who is truly in charge of his business!

RULE #4

Separate Your Cost of Sales And Know
How Much You Need To Break Even

As I hinted at earlier, there's a quick but super effective hack you should do with your P&L statement that will seriously help you navigate the finances in your business. To get a much clearer picture on your business performance, I strongly recommend you make a small adjustment to the way your Profit & Loss Statement reads on your accounting system.

As I mentioned, the default layout for most accounting systems regard materials and labour as normal operational 'Expenses'. In trades businesses though, these are very significant costs that are directly related to the job. So, my hack is to allocate materials and labour to Cost of Sales.

You can do this in the back end of your accounting system. Simply ask your accountant to do it for you or give me a bell and I can tweak it for you. It is very important to separate these expenses from one another. There are a few different reasons for it, but the number one reason is so that we can work out your "Break Even Number".

That is, the MINIMUM amount of work you must do to break even in your business (or not earn a profit but not go backwards, either). Plus, while not an exact science, we can also start to predict what your profit will be based on the income coming in. Let me explain.

Expenses (your overhead ones) are normally quite consistent. You have got your rent, your insurance, your phone bill, your business car loan, etc... they're usually fixed costs, right? So, they are normally about the same each month. If you don't believe me, just go through your own P&L Statement and see for yourself. This monthly expense number should be about the same (give or take a smidge) each month.

Whereas the Cost of Sales CAN'T be predicted each month because it's directly linked to the amount of work you do, and you don't have that income number ahead of time. But – and this is a key point here – Cost of Sales is still a fairly predictable percentage because it's directly linked to the amount of work you do. For example, if you have 50% more work, you can expect site labour and materials to be 50% higher as well, right? Twice the work, twice the amount of costs to get the job done. Make sense?

So, if we can reasonably predict our expenses AND our Cost of Sales... what does that mean?

Well, it means we can come up with a nifty calculation that lets us PREDICT how much income we need to "Break Even"... AND see what kind of profit we'll get when we bring in a certain amount of income.

To demonstrate this, let's look at our electrical company again.

Based on the information we filled in on our REAL Financial Performance Sheet, we can see that our percentage for the Cost of Sales is 52% and our REAL expenses average monthly cost is $9,844.

Once we know these two numbers, we're set! Simply bang them in my free Breakeven & Profit Calculator, and the tool will run the numbers for you.

Basically, anything in brackets means you are running your profit at a LOSS.

The moment the brackets disappear is your BREAK EVEN point.

Breakeven & Profit Target Calculator

| Average Cost of Sales % | 52% | Enter average information from Historical sheet |
| Average Expenses per month | $ 9,844 | Enter average information from Historical sheet |

Sales	Cost of Sales % of Sales	Gross Profit	Average Expenses	Profit
$ 6,000	52%	$ 2,880	$ 9,844	$ (6,964)
$ 8,000	52%	$ 3,840	$ 9,844	$ (6,004)
$ 10,000	52%	$ 4,800	$ 9,844	$ (5,044)
$ 12,000	52%	$ 5,760	$ 9,844	$ (4,084)
$ 14,000	52%	$ 6,720	$ 9,844	$ (3,124)
$ 16,000	52%	$ 7,680	$ 9,844	$ (2,164)
$ 18,000	52%	$ 8,640	$ 9,844	$ (1,204)
$ 20,000	52%	$ 9,600	$ 9,844	$ (244)
$ 22,000	52%	$ 10,560	$ 9,844	$ 716
$ 24,000	52%	$ 11,520	$ 9,844	$ 1,676
$ 26,000	52%	$ 12,480	$ 9,844	$ 2,636
$ 28,000	52%	$ 13,440	$ 9,844	$ 3,596
$ 30,000	52%	$ 14,400	$ 9,844	$ 4,556
$ 32,000	52%	$ 15,360	$ 9,844	$ 5,516
$ 34,000	52%	$ 16,320	$ 9,844	$ 6,476
$ 36,000	52%	$ 17,280	$ 9,844	$ 7,436
$ 38,000	52%	$ 18,240	$ 9,844	$ 8,396
$ 40,000	52%	$ 19,200	$ 9,844	$ 9,356
$ 42,000	52%	$ 20,160	$ 9,844	$ 10,316
$ 44,000	52%	$ 21,120	$ 9,844	$ 11,276
$ 46,000	52%	$ 22,080	$ 9,844	$ 12,236

BREAKEVEN POINT!

You need to do $22,000 in Sales (Work) for the month to breakeven in your business!

Looking at the "Sales" column, you can discover how much money you need to bring in (from the work you do) to earn a particular amount of profit. Using the above example, we can see that we need bring in $22,000 for the month to "breakeven" in our business (or more accurately, you'll bring in a grand total of $716 in profit.) Anything less than $22,000 a month means you will be running your business at a LOSS.

We can also see here that if we had a Profit target for the month of $10,000, we'd need to bring in $42,000 in Sales/Work.

Super Note!! – Trick for young players. This is the accounting breakeven and is covered a bit further on in the book.

If for example you have equipment loans or a tax debt you are paying off, you need additional profit. Technically paying off loans is a balance sheet entry and hence not included in the P&L. So if you pay say $8k/month in loan repayments, your break even is now $30k/month ($22+8)

Rule #5

Master The Cash Gap Strategy! (This Is The Best Way To Get Paid On Time & Chase Up Late Payers)

A 'Cash Gap' is the time between paying for something and not getting the money back. For example, you buy materials and pay your supplier on Day 1. You then get your tradies to do the job on Day 7... but you don't get your money from your customer until Day 30.

There's a gap between when YOU must pay for something and when you get paid for it, right? This means the money is in your customers bank and not yours. This is not good. You don't really want a gap at all. What happens when customers are late in paying? Well, the gap is widened, and this is definitely not good!

The Cash Gap Strategy is having a system in place so your admin staff can follow up with unpaid invoices so you get your money as quickly as possible.

You need to set some actions around your own Cash Gap Strategy – that is, how you're going to go about getting the money owed to you ASAP. This sounds simple enough, but so many tradie owners are missing this vital step. Some owners I speak with tell me that their accounting software automatically sends email reminders to their clients about late payments, but that doesn't cut it. Why? Well, how many emails do YOU get a day? Stacks, right? Or more than you probably want, at the very least.

Most of us are already overwhelmed. Most of us are already getting too many spam emails. So when we see anything that looks remotely close to spam, we don't open the damn thing, do we? Well, this is probably happening to your customers when they receive an email that's been automatically sent from your accounting system. Your Cash Gap Strategy has to include phone calls as well as email. Even do the old snail mail if you really have to.

Plus, a brilliant Cash Gap strategy must be written up and placed where everyone can see it. It needs to spell out EXACTLY what happens when an account is 7 days, 14 days, and 21 days overdue. Is a phone call made? Is an email sent? It needs to be a specific task given to a specific staff member as a key part of their role.

Check out a really great example of a Cash Gap Strategy below:

THE CASH GAP STRATEGY: The Proven System

When	TO DO	✉	📞
After They Say "Yes" To Working With You	Ask for signed order with Terms & Conditions (T&C'S) Get verbal and written acceptance of order that outlines your terms Verbally mention terms and debt collection process	Send T&C for them to sign	Verbally ask if they are good with paying on time and OK with the terms Example: *"My terms are XYZ. My payment times are XYZ, which means I expect to be paid within X days of doing the job. Are you okay with that?"*
When You Invoice	Clearly state the due date and what happens 14 and 21 days from date of invoice if it remains unpaid You might be able to state 2% per month overdue fee? (depends on your industry)	Send invoice via email / hard copy (tell the customer which one you will do.)	
Overdue + 0 Days	Resend invoice or statement	Resend invoice or statement via email	
Overdue + 7 Days	Resend invoice or statement	Resend invoice or statement via email	Call customer – use Script 1
Overdue + 14 Days	Resend invoice or statement	Resend invoice or statement via email (and hard copy if appropriate) with the following included: *Your account is now more than 2 weeks overdue.* *A late fee has been applied (if applicable).* *Please contact us immediately to discuss.*	Call customer – use Script 2
Overdue + 21 Days	Resend invoice or statement via email)	Resend invoice or statement via email (and hard copy if appropriate) with the following included: *A late fee has been applied (if applicable)* *Please contact us immediately to discuss* *This is my final reminder. Our debt collector will now be engaged to recover debts within 3 days from the date of this email/letter*	Call customer – use Script 3
Overdue + 24 Days	Proceed with debt collection		

THE CASH GAP STRATEGY: The Phone Scripts

SCRIPT 1	SCRIPT 2	SCRIPT 3
When you TALK to the customer:	**When you TALK to the customer:**	**When you TALK to the customer:**
Hi, are you keeping busy...?	*Hi, are you keeping busy...?*	*Hi, we need to talk to you about your account right now.*
So, we just need to fix up the account now....	*We need to fix up your account from 2 weeks ago.*	*Currently it is 3 weeks overdue. Would you like to do it right now over the phone or transfer it right now and send me the receipt?*
Would you like to do it right now over the phone?	*Are we able to do that now...*	
If not now, when?	*Would you like to do it right now over the phone?*	*If not right now..... When?*
(Take notes of what they say and when to follow up – you can do this in your online system)	*If not right now.... When?*	*Just so that you know, we have a late fee that we don't really want to add on....*
	Just so that you know, we have a late fee that we don't really want to add on...	*If you get it in in the next day or so we will not apply it.*
	If you get it in in the next day or so we will not apply it.	*Just so you know, my accounts lady will send this off to our debt collector within 3 days....*
	(Take notes of what they say and when to follow up)	*Also, we are pulling guys off site as of Friday and prioritising other work.*
		(Take notes of what they say and when to follow up)
When you get their MESSAGE BANK:	**When you get their MESSAGE BANK:**	**When you get their MESSAGE BANK:**
Hi, I just have a question about your account, can you please call us back today?	*Hi, just letting you know that your account from 2 weeks ago is overdue.*	*Hi, just letting you know that your account from 3 weeks ago is overdue. This is now an urgent matter.*
(Take note that you called them)	*Just so that you know, we have an overdue fee that should be applied right now, but if you call us back in the next 2 days, we won't apply it.*	*Please call me back as soon as you can.*
	(Take note that you called them)	*Thank you.*
		(Take note that you called them)

You can also find an "Outstanding Debtors Report" (a list of all the customers who owe you money) in your accounting system. I strongly suggest getting this report automatically sent to you (and the staff member in charge of the follow up) – once a week. This can be done in both QuickBooks and Xero. Note: Just looking at your Xero dashboard and seeing how much there is overdue doesn't cut it! You need to know who, how much, and how long overdue.

This way, you'll be across it (at least initially anyway) and the staff member responsible for managing late payers will know where everything currently stands, who to talk to, and how to send the outstanding balance off to a debt collector if needed.

Quick Tips On How To Get Paid Quicker!

- The "Cash Gap Strategy" sounds obvious, but the biggest tip to minimise your cash gap and get paid quicker is to get invoices out fast.

- If it's a little job, collect money as soon as you complete it.

- If it's a mid-size job, make sure invoices are sent out weekly.

- For larger-build construction-type jobs, send invoices monthly.

- If the job is over a long period and payments will be, say, 30 days, make sure you do work in progress claims.

RULE #6

Know When To Pay Yourself

One of the most frequently asked questions I get is, *"How much do I pay myself?"*

I've got a client who's running a successful three man business that does bathroom extensions for occupational therapists. His business is quite profitable, although he runs it with high working capital (there's more than enough money available to meet the short-term needs of the business). To give you an idea: he has more than $100,000 in his bank account. This amount of money isn't really needed. His process for paying himself? It's this: he takes money if he wants it.

So clearly, he's not an overspender, he just doesn't know how much to pay himself! Then there's the flipside of this – I once met with someone who had only just started his business and he was already paying himself a very handsome wage. Something like this can very quickly strangle the business. Not to mention, I always hear new clients say they "could make more money working for someone else"! Obviously, the truth of this will vary from role to role – but this is not something you want to be saying if you're an owner who's going to all the effort (and taking all the risks!) to run your own business.

You want to make sure you get a return for this risk but also not strangling the business and not giving it enough cash to grow.

How much should you pay yourself?

In an ideal situation, I recommend you pay yourself what someone else in your role would be getting paid. If there is leftover profit, you can take a dividend every quarter or so. This way you will have the confidence you are better off than having a job, and the business is genuinely profitable and will have a value to sell one day. (Cha ching!)

If you are unable to pay this amount, please just make it a fixed regular amount that you're happy with so that you can start to live your life based on this amount. The only reason that you would pay yourself less than working for someone else is because you want to grow the business, or it gives you a lifestyle improvement.

"Should I pay myself a wage or a drawing?" When it comes to paying yourself a drawing or a wage, I am a little indifferent. A wage forces you to pay some super and can give you some work cover, which is a good thing. Drawings might give you some more flexibility at tax time... so you need to work out what best works for you and your needs. That said, this is a great question for you accountant.

Why You Should Run Your Business Accounts LOW.

As a continuation of the story above, I recommend running your business accounts low rather than the example of $100K in the bank account above. Why? Having a large sum of money in your business accounts will give you a false sense of security. You may become nonchalant about when you get invoices out. You may wait until invoices are overdue before sending them (or payment reminders). Perhaps to the point that it gets too long, and you may never get the money! And you think, "She'll be right, I've got money in the bank." Keeping your bank accounts low will keep you motivated to collect money owed. It will give you the sense of urgency to get things done and out the door. It will make you 'hungry'… and hungry people always prioritise getting fed.

Case in point: one of my tradie clients has done exactly as I suggested. He takes enough cash out to pay himself personally and leaves his business accounts low. The result? Now, we continually analyse the profitability of the business and look for ways to make more money! Should he be increasing labour rates? How much should he be allowing for overhead? Is he billing enough hours out? Is he making money on each job? It creates unending attention to improve the business and keep your finger on the pulse.

I'm making a profit, so where's all my money?

It's common for me to meet business owners who can see they're making a profit on their Profit & Loss Statement but are still short on cash. Why is this happening?

This can get quite complex, but you need to understand it. From my experience with trades, there are a couple reasons why cash is usually short. These are:

1. Invoices haven't been paid. The cash is 'missing' because it is literally missing. Start chasing up the payments immediately

2. There's an increasing or a high level of stock. Your money's sitting on the floor in your workshop!

3. These two are quite easy to understand. But there is a third one:

4. Loan Payments.

The third one that's more difficult to understand is loan repayments. Loans are listed on the Balance Sheet and don't appear on the Profit & Loss Statement.

If everything else is equal, if you had $8,000/month in loan repayments, you would need to make a profit GREATER THAN $8,000 to be cash break even.

This is on top of your normal Breakeven number. Although a bit tricky to understand, please just know that it really is possible to go broke while making a profit! So keep track of ALL your numbers and get someone on board to help you if you need extra coaching!

ACTION ITEM

- If you don't have an accounting system set up, get one today (latest on Friday!) – great examples are Xero, MYOB or Quickbooks

- Look at your Profit & Loss Statement in your accounting system (and do this REGULARLY!)

- Update your Profit & Loss Statement so that 'Materials and Labour' expenses are included as Cost of Sale items (get your bookkeeper to do this for you if you need a hand. I can also do it for you if you want.)

- Print out a hard copy of my 'The Cash Gap Strategy' and put it in your lunchroom/office – available at www.wealthytradie.com.au/freebies

- Fill out the free REAL Financial Performance spreadsheet now – get it for free at www.wealthytradie.com.au/freebies

READ ON....

Chapter Six

Stump #4: SERVICE DELIVERY

Now that we've gone through our first three "Stumps" of building a sturdy foundation for your business (Destination, Time and Financials) It's time for our fourth and final one! Remember – just like our chair needs four legs to stay standing, so too does our business!

Let's be frank. You're already great on the tools, so you don't need me to tell you how to do your job. 'Service delivery' in this context isn't just about how you perform the job to best take care of your customers. It's about how you are RUNNING your business at every stage of the customer journey. This includes:

- workflow process
- managing staff to ensure they are performing the work at a consistent, high standard for customers

- ensuring your business is optimised to run as smoothly and efficiently as possible.

And the best way to master your Service Delivery pretty much comes down to four things – nailing your "QEWS":

- **Quality**
- **Expectations**
- **Workflow**
- **Systems**

While this is just a fancy way to remember something pretty darn important, what we're tackling here in this section is all about quality assurance, establishing expectations for your team (and for your customers), coming up with (and sticking to!) workflow processes and – the game changer – bringing in a job management system into your business.

QUALITY

When I say 'Quality' what I mean here is Quality Assurance (QA). This is a step-by-step process to complete a job so it's at the highest standard. This is where technology (like a job management system) can really come into play as you can include a QA Checklist – a 'tick off' list of everything required to complete the job.

Getting the guys to tick off each box when they're actually at the job so nothing gets missed. To do this, you'd program a form in your job management system and have your tradies take an iPhone on site where they can simply tick a 'yes' or 'no' box, and take a photo when they're done so you proof the job's been done and at a standard that's representative of your company.

This has a double benefit as it doesn't just make sure the quality is up to scratch, it safeguards you if a customer calls up and asks, "When are you going to come back and finish the job? when you know your guys have already done it! You would simply look at your system, see that, yep, So-and-So completed the job on 'X' date and – look at that – there's even a picture there of the completed job!

Even if you aren't taking advantage of the power of technology in your business just yet, it's still vitally important to create this Quality Assurance process. Some tradies might opt to capture the process in a notebook, and then type it up once they're back at home or in the office... but they always should have a clear process to follow, especially if you are relying on your workers to do a good job, and you're not there to personally tick off on the job. You'll see an example below to highlight this, but it's important to capture the MAIN parts of a job.

There's no limit to how many 'tick boxes' to include, however, you do want to make sure your guys will follow through on it. It depends on the business, but sometimes if it's too long, they might be less likely to stick to it.

Here's an example QA checklist for a business installing split airconditioning units:

- √ All pipework clipped and supported to wall, including insulations
- √ All pipework pressure tested
- √ Pipework evacuated prior to charging
- √ Condensate drain run to drain point
- √ Unit secured firmly to brackets or concrete
- √ Manuals left behind in switch board
- √ Remove all rubbish

EXPECTATIONS

It's vitally important that your staff are aware of your expectations for onsite work – this includes expectations on quality as well as what to do on a job and how to leave a site. Typically, you want to write out these expectations in a document and give this document to any new tradie who starts with you. During their training, you'd go through each expectation line by line, so they are very clear on how to conduct themselves and their standard of work.

During this time, you'd give them the opportunity to ask you any questions, flesh out anything they aren't sure of, and ultimately get to the point where you're both on the same page with what needs to be done, no excuses. You'd give them this sheet to take home and reread over.

Here's an example list of expectations for a maintenance electrician:

Arrival (Site Techs)

- Do not park in the driveway unless instructed by the homeowner/tenant. If there is no street parking available, request permission via a direct phone call.
- Take hand tools, work mats and vac from car to front door.
- Ring the doorbell or knock. When greeting a client, introduce yourself with your name and apprentice's name.
- Explain to the client what the work order states and if this is correct. If there is any discrepancy, advise that you will contact your supervisor/agent to seek direction for any variations.
- Take pictures of the site you are working on prior to any works being performed. Taking particular notice if there is any pre-existing damage and advise the client/tenant as soon as you become aware.

During (Site Techs)

- Place the work mat in a suitable location ensuring no trip hazard is created. Take time to consider if children are present and what is the best location for tools.
- If power isolation is required during the works, please advise the tenant that isolation is required and that they should save any work on their computers and that they will lose internet and possibly hot water if it's gas. Ask if now is a suitable time.
- If client/tenant is present, no inappropriate language should be used. Consider your surroundings and keep voices down if people are sleeping or unwell. Avoid loud singing and taking phone calls during work. If the office calls, please leave the property and answer the phone outside.
- Vacuum as you go to avoid spreading waste, dust, and dirt throughout the site.
- If works cannot be completed due to parts being required, create a task in job management system and allocate accordingly.
- Once works have been completed, demonstrate to the homeowner or tenant what has been performed and confirm their acceptance.
- Take pictures of completed works from within your app.

- Complete job card, ensuring all labour and materials are captured. If material is required to be ordered, make notes with as much detail as possible and create task to order.

Leaving (Site Techs)

- Ensure the manhole is in place, roof tiles or sheets reinstalled, all circuits energised.
- Remove all rubbish.
- Apply company sticker to switch board, security panel or comms rack depending on what you worked on.

WORKFLOW

To make sure your service delivery is as smooth and efficient as possible, it's important to map out your entire workflow process – that is a step-by-step flowchart of exactly what to do for a particular task. You would use this as a training document for new staff so they know exactly what to do for specific tasks, as well as a reference document if you're having trouble getting staff members stick to your preferred process. You don't need it to look as polished as the below document if you're not there yet – at the most basic level, please just scribble it out. You would do this for each workflow process in your business. Here's an Example Workflow Process – Incoming Service Call For A Plumbing Business:

1
- Collect customer details
- Collect job details
- Enter into Fergus (job management system)

2
- Explain pricing terms (COD - Cash On Delivery for new customers and small jobs)
- Give estimate/budget over the phone
- Ask for photo (if it will be useful)

3a
- If smaller job: complete steps in 3a. If bigger job, follow steps in 3b instead.
- Book in time (with 1 hour window)
- Call or SMS when on the way
- Ask the customer if they are running late or something changes to please let you know
- If you are running late, call the customer directly

3b
- If bigger job: SMS on Sunday night to confirm

4
- Arrive onsite / Inspect
- Mention payment terms again

5
- Buy materials (if required)
- Use job address as reference with suppliers
- Enter photo of docket into Fergus

6
- Installation work incl. Remove rubbish

7
- Confirm work with customer before leaving (demonstartions, etc)
- Make sure they are happy

8
- Take payment and send invoice
- Send receipt (next day)

9
- SMS for next job
- If finishing earlier than expected, call owner with 1 hour notice.

SYSTEMS

In the early stages of running a business, the owner
needs to do it all — win the work, do the work
and invoice the work. This quickly leads to long
nights spent doing quotes, invoices and account
reconciliation (all the unfun admin stuff... after
hours.) There is barely enough time to do all that, let
alone think about proper job planning, maximising
your staff output or increasing job profitability.

An important evolutionary stage for any small
business owner is the point when they STOP
DOING EVERYTHING and instead focus their time
on the right things and start leveraging systems for
the rest of it.

If you haven't heard it before, there's a common
saying out there that "System" stands for: Saves
You Serious Time, Energy and Money... and
nothing could be more true.

Just the word 'system' can send people into a right
ol' spin. Navigating the tech side of your business
can be tough and it's actually one of the top reasons
people choose to speak with a business coach like
me in the first place.We regularly help clients deal
with the curveball of choices out there and decide

which systems best suit them and their business.
For trade and service-based businesses, a proper Job
Management System can be one of the MOST useful
tools in your business. Game-changingly useful. The
"Why the heck didn't I do it earlier?" kind of useful.
At their core, a job management system help
business owners prepare and track quotes, schedule
and manage jobs, schedule and manage staff, make
invoicing easier and run reports to make informed
(and better) business decisions.

"Which Job Management System is best for my business?"

As with all systems and technology whether it's a
Customer Relationship Management (CRM) system,
accounting package, inventory management or
job management system. There are many options
available and they all have differing levels of
features, pricing and processing complexity. There
seems to be another one added to the list "every
week" too, so I won't nit-pick between them all here,
but rather give you an overview of what to look for.

Some questions to consider when deciding which
job management system is best for you and your
business:

- How easy will it work with my current systems?
- What changes will be required to the way we currently do things?
- How much training is needed to learn how to use this new system effectively?
- What will I actually use and need in real-world scenarios?
- Is the solution that's right for my business NOW going to suit my needs and budget in the future?
- Is all of that worth the cost of my time and money?

Now, with over 11 years of coaching many businesses across multiple industries, it's fair to say I've seen my share of job management systems. So, I can pass on a couple of "recommendations" – though please understand that I'm NOT incentivised by any of the software companies to do so. I've just found these particular systems to work well for my tradie clients (at the time of writing).

Obviously, there are dozens of job management systems on the market, and you need to be mindful of your own business needs and costs.

The 6 Most Common Job Management Systems for Tradies:

- Fergus
- simPRO
- AroFlo
- ServiceM8
- Tradify
- BuilderTREND
- Asana
- Monday

Some business owners don't buy the systems simply because they're not sure which one is best for their individual business needs. For example, simPRO is known to be great for quoted work, but Fergus is better for charge-up work. Some are great for little businesses that are only made up of one or two employees. Do your research to find the best one for your business or speak to a business coach who can guide you in this area without the sales pitch.

It's also important to note that businesses do actually outgrow their job management systems. So if you're just starting, it's far better to get one suitable for where you want your business to be in the future, not where you currently are. The better ones have far more powerful reporting capabilities that can actually work out what billable rates are, where the higher-profit jobs are, and other vitally important information.

A good job management system will help you find this data a whole lot easier. You might even get some of them to start paying you $40 a month to implement them into your business. Yes, they offer incentives so you'll pick their system over someone else's – always come back to what you most need, both today and when your business grows, as well as the normal cost outside promo offers.

Chapter Seven

THE BUILDING

Making The Money!

Now that we've laid our critical foundations, it's time to get excited because we're taking things up a notch. That's right. The slab's laid, the thing's nice solid (and level), and now it's time to chuck a nice-looking house on top that does all the things nice looking houses are supposed to do.

Here we're diving deep on building your actual business. First, we refined it so we got you out of chaos and back into the driver's seat of control (it feels good, doesn't it – no more drowning in your day-to-day)... and now it's time to...

... Make Some Money!

This section is all about "making the moolah", "bringing home the bacon" and "reeling it in" – so if you like the sounds of making money, then you'll learn a thing or two over our time together.

Obviously, you can't just read a book and make money in your business – like all great things in life, it will require some ACTION on your part.

But knowledge is always where the riches start. Learn first and then act on the information because what I'm about to walk you through is the 'meat and potatoes' that will help fund that dream lifestyle of yours we've been banging on about.

Let's take your trades business and turn it into a machine that makes you money. This can only happen after you've laid the correct foundations first. Anyone who tells you otherwise is trying to sell you something. We want to make sure the success sticks.

We'll be focusing on Five Key Areas:

1. Dream Customer – This customer pays you more money, is someone you "click with" and will tell their friends and family how great you and your company is. Basically, I'm going to give you the strategy and tools to find this dream customer, keep them and pivot your business so you only work with customers you LOVE (and who love you).

2. Marketing – Marketing is the art and science of getting more work. I'll explain how to best promote your trades business in the most cost-effective way possible that'll generate higher quality work!

3. Sales – Don't freak out… I'm not going to turn you into a shark. (We all hate those slick guys in suits who are full of it.) There is a way to "sell" that's 100% genuine – and by "sell" I simply mean making sure someone says 'yes' to working with you and not 'yes' to the guy around the corner who charges more and doesn't do as good a job. The definition of work is someone paying you to do something helpful for them. This section is just making sure potential customers know how you can help them so you get more work and they stay happy.

4. Profitability – No one goes into business to go broke. We want to make sure your business is not only creating a profit for you but is also making enough cash that it funds your dream lifestyle. We'll get you ahead of the game on pricing, productivity, billing rules and – the one that trips a lot of you up – getting super clear on what the real cost of labour is.

5. Team – It has been said that the greatest asset in business is your people. So how do you build a hardworking team that loves to show up and get the job done, and who will also work with you for the long term? Whether it's your tradie, a new apprentice or an admin worker, let's get your team pumped and proud to do an outstanding job for you.

Chapter Eight

DREAM CUSTOMER

How To Attract Them

Have you ever heard of something called "The Pareto principle"? Many moons ago, there was a very smart guy called Vilfredo Pareto who noticed that approximately 80% of the land in Italy was owned by 20% of the population. He realised only a very small portion of people owned the greatest chunk of the country. Anyway, he started to notice this trend everywhere and came up with this whizz-bang mathematical model to describe what he was seeing. He worked out that 80% of outcomes come from only 20% of causes.

Said another way: about 20% of what you do, will give you 80% of your results.

This is true in EVERY aspect of your business
That's why we get you focused on working "on" the
business as this is the 20% that'll give you maximum
results. Nowhere is this more impactful than when
it comes to your customers. Think about what the
principle is saying: about 80% of your profits come
from the top 20% of your customers.

Holy smokes – it's a lot, right?

So, imagine if you ONLY worked with those Top
20% of customers. Things would significantly
change for you and your business, right?

Many tradie owners tell me they want to grow but
they don't want NEW customers. Their phone rings,
and they're busy with all the wrong ones. They're not
targeting the ideal customer that fits well with their
skills, their profit margin, the location, and the type
of work that they are really great at.

Here's the truth: Stop focusing on customers who
simply call and start focusing more on the types
of customers you really want to work with. The
customers who will play by your rules. You'll end
up much happier, be more profitable, and have much
more appropriate customers for the equipment,
skills, and staff you have.

A Dream Customer is a customer who pays you more money, is someone you "click with" and who will tell their friends and family how great you and your company are. Oh – and the big one – they'll work with you again and again and again. A repeat client who you love working with is a business owner's *Dream Customer*!

There are a few 'tricks' to attract your dream customer to your business, but here's the "Give it to me quick" snapshot:

- Know what you're the best at and focus on it
- Rank your customers and CHOOSE jobs
- Increase repeat customers

Know what you're the best at and focus on it
This is pretty simple but so overlooked, it's ridiculous. Ask yourself:

- What is your business really good at?
- What are you KNOWN for?
- What do people say, "You're the best at...."?
- WHERE are you making the most money in your business?

For example, let's say you're a service and repair plumber who's hired for all sorts of repair and maintenance jobs (commercial and homes)... what's your MAIN type of work?

Are you fixing broken toilets all the time – maybe for commercial offices – and, for whatever reason, this also happens to be highly profitable for you? If so, you are the *"Office Toilet Plumber"* This is what you become what known for.

Although this is a very basic example you would advertise yourself with this in mind and focus on getting the commercial jobs in older buildings where the plumbing's old and more likely to be buggered. That's where the money is, and that's where your *Dream Customers* are. On the flipside, if you do a lot of toilet repairs but you bloody hate doing them because the work sucks, they're not worth much and those types of customers normally complain and pay late then consider passing on the work.

This might seem counter-intuitive to knock back work but here's what a lot of tradie owners overlook. The time you spend doing a cheap job for a less-than-ideal customer is better spent going directly after your *Dream Customer* who'll pay you more money to do the work you prefer to do!

Remember the 80/20 rule. And always remember you've only got one crack at things with the time you have. The work you want is there just chase after it. Here's another key point: your *Dream*

Customer wants what you're good at! They want to pay you to solve their trades problem for them. Therefore make sure they know you exist, can find you easily, and are confident that you can do the work for them. The quickest and easiest way to do this is to know what you're the best at and focus on it!

Rank Your Customers

Let me say it again – cutting some of those not-so-great customers loose will let you focus your attention on the BEST type of customer instead. Think about it this way. Would you rather do cheaper work with customers who are a pain in the arse and don't pay you on time, or would you rather do the higher-profit jobs with customers who praise you for the job, pay you on time and then go on to tell all their friends and family about you?

Err… It's a stupid question, right?! Of course you'd pick the better customer. It's a no brainer. Why on earth do we approach our business like we must work with every man and his dog just to earn a living? The best work with the best. And the secret? The best can ALWAYS tell who the best is!

This is why it's important to RANK your customers. You need to be crystal clear on how your current

customers stack up – who are you working with
that's a great fit for your business? Who, on the other
hand, is simply sucking the lifeblood out of you,
your staff and your business? Who would you pick
if you had to work with a similar 'type' of customer
moving forward?

The best way to rank your customers is to literally
do just that – give them a grade of "A, B, C or D" as
shown below.

A – GRADE CLIENTS Amazing!	- Raving Fans
	- Refers others
	- Pays on time
	- Never questions invoices
	- Repeat customer
	- Great to work with
B – GRADE CLIENTS Basic	- Reasonable volume of sales
	- Ok with your service
C – GRADE CLIENTS Can just Deal With	- Expect you to jump with little notice
	- Questions every invoice and breakdown
	- Wants cheaper prices
	- Slow payer
D – GRADE CLIENTS Avoid!	- Too hard to work with
	- Often lose money on jobs
	- Staff don't like working for them
	- Late payers

Anyone who is an A-Grade customer is your *Dream Customer*, they are the cream of the crop – and you want these people as customers for life. You also want to attract MORE of these same types of people. Think about who you are marking with top grades and see if there are patterns or common traits emerging. Take note because these are signs that will help you identify your dream customer in future and you can actually use this exact information in your marketing to attract a similar type of person.

An example is Pete who owns a cabinetry business and targets higher end jobs. Through careful targeting of builders, he has three builders that give his business about half of all their work. These three builders all have similar characteristics:

1. They give him all the good work
2. It's easy for Pete to overdeliver on his service
3. They don't ask him to compete.

For example, Pete is asked to quote every high-end job and they don't ask anyone else for a quote. Pete identifies issues with the drawings and makes suggestions to improve the job at the same price and does a great job (this means these same A-Grade customers LOVE him!) The builders are great with communication and are easy to work with on site.

Best of all, they always pay invoices on time without question.

You MUST focus your time, energy and efforts on the A and B Grade customers... NOT the C and D! These last two you should look to phase out as your customers especially the D's, they have got to go! Another tradie will be willing to take them on. Set your own standards higher. D customers are not worth the headache.

On this point, also start choosing the work you want to do and, importantly, the jobs that have been demonstrated to be more profitable for you. Many tradie owners get trapped in the "feast then famine" mindset where they're worried if they knock back work, they won't get it again.

Mate, you need to realise that this simply is not true. You're wasting your time with the tiny, cheap jobs. Honestly you need to shake up your mindset here because when you say 'Yes' to a lousy job, you're literally saying 'No' to the work you actually want!

We all only have limited time, resources and energy so spend yours where it matters and on what will give you the most 'bang for buck'. Plus, life is too short to be dealing with customers (and work!) you don't even like!

Increase Repeat Customers

I hinted at it earlier, but did you know that often the best type of customer is the one who has already worked with you?

I suggest looking under the bonnet at your existing customers and trying to increase repeat business from them especially the A and B grade customers.

Why? Well, it has been proven that *Repeat Customers* those who have already done business with you) are far more likely to:

- Spend more money with you
- Promote your business
- Buy more from you without you having to convince them you're the man for the job

In fact, repeat customers not only refer more people to a business than anyone else – they refer more people to a business when they've bought MORE from your company! Repeat customers grow even more in value over time. Who doesn't love free marketing? Plus, it costs way less to keep a current customer than to bring on a new one. Unless you know for sure that your new customers are going to be those 'A and B Grade' customers it's worth looking at your current top customers and seeing what you can do to make them want to do more business with you.

I will go into this in a lot more detail when we get to our 'Marketing' section, but here are a few 'quick wins' that you can do right away in your trades business to increase repeat customers:

TIP #1: Set up reminder calls/SMS/letters.

After you've completed the job, set up a reminder system to check back in with the customer to see how it's all going. They'll love that you have taken the time to check in with them, and you'll also get the opportunity to see if there is another way you could help them. Even if the job's all good and they don't require your service elsewhere, they will remember that you called them up.

If they do need more work, you'll be front of mind. *"Oh yeah, I remember the guy who called to check in… he was pretty good actually… I'll give him a ring."* People care about the small details and if they feel like you really care about them, they will be more than happy to do business with you again.

Example SMS

Hi John, just letting you know that your gas heater is due for its 2 yearly service. If you would like to book it in, please call Ben, North West Air conditioning 0123456789.

TIP #2: Leave Your Brand Behind

There are some obvious ways to "Leave your brand behind" at the job like leaving a magnet on the fridge or a couple of stickers and business cards on the kitchen bench, but there's actually some interesting "out of the box" ways to really stand out and be remembered after you have left the jobsite. One is an engraved floor tile! A company I worked with actually engraves a tile and puts it the cleaning cupboard after they're done with the job. Likewise, there's a painter who paints a stencil of his logo, again in the cleaning cupboard.

The script might go something like:
"It's been great painting your house. Do you mind if we put a little branding in your cleaning cupboard so you can remember who we are? It will be out of sight, but if there's ever an issue or someone asks who painted your house, you won't have to reach far to find us."

This repeat customer strategy is obviously a bit non-standard, but it's great idea to start brainstorming unique ways to 'stand out from the crowd'… permanently. We're getting away from the old refrigerator magnet that gets thrown out or a business card that gets lost.

TIP #3: Stay in touch... in a way the CUSTOMER likes.

When it comes to repeat business, I often get feedback from my clients who want to know if they must email their customers regular newsletters. This newsletter strategy can really work for certain businesses, but when it comes to a tradie business... perhaps not so much. You've got to think about it from the customers' point of view. Do they really want to come home from work and read an email from their plumber? I mean, what would this newsletter say that would be of interest to them?

You always have to think about how the person on the RECEIVING end of your marketing would feel about it. In some instances, a newsletter could work for a tradie business as long as it is valuable to the customer, or something they get benefit from (even if it's just enjoyment).

Remember, we're all busy – and so are your customers. Always come back to the 80/20 principle – you could write the same email to every single client you've ever worked with... or you could use that time to handpick the 4 best clients and send them something thoughtful in the post (or better yet hand deliver it if they're close by!)

As a side note: if you DO go down the email newsletter route, please make sure you are using an online job system that lets you send out one bulk email to all your customers, so you're not wasting precious time sending an email one by one.

I want to also tell you about Tom. He's a plumber who actually writes a Christmas card to his customers every year. At first, this might sound a little strange... but think about it: Who doesn't want to receive a Christmas card? It's thoughtful and lovely and not too over the top.

Guess what? Tom is known as the *go to plumber* for Manifold and Newtown (two suburbs side-by-side here in Geelong). The act of writing a personalised Christmas card to that small group makes him even more popular. If the area you service is large, this obviously wouldn't work but it should get you thinking. It always comes down to: What would make me stand out from the crowd? What isn't going to cost me stacks? What would the customer enjoy? What would remind them to want to do business with me again?

Chapter Nine

MARKETING

Your Tradie Business

Tradie owners don't seem to like marketing. They find it a challenge. Often starting out with something easy like Facebook and think, "Right. I'm now having a crack at marketing…" Don't do this.

Instead focus on what will get you the best results in the shortest amount of time possible. If you work with builders, you only need a handful of customers, right? So all you need to do is target those customers DIRECTLY. That means literally picking up the phone, knocking on the door and going in to the actual business for an actual human chat (What happened to those…?).

It's a big challenge for so many business owners to *allocate the time* to identify their dream customer and then go after them but it's worth it. If you knew that taking a short-term hit on your time would lead to great, well-paying (and likely repeat) work, wouldn't that justify the time spent? Note my purposely used wording — 'allocate the time' – there's a big difference between having time and making time for what's important. I want to share with you a little story to highlight this point.

I know a business owner who openly says he hasn't had much education. He left school in Year 8 and his partner left school in Year 7. He told me that neither of them can read or write that well but their roofing business is turning over $5 million a year.

Impressed, I asked him, "Where did you get all your customers from?" He was a bit vague, but said something like: *"In the beginning, I called or met with several builders. All I did was show them how good we were and now we get endless repeat work from them."* He met with the builders. He did a great job. He got heaps of repeat business. The cycle continued and now he turns over $5 mill a year.

Isn't that simplicity just beautiful? There's all the bells and whistles and the latest marketing education and "tricks" out there, and this guy simply jumped on the phone and now his business is booming. He's the one in 100 people who actually knocked on the door... and by doing so, he talked to the exact customer he wants! It's quite impressive.

Another simple marketing tip I've found that works well, particularly in the residential space — no matter if it's electrical, plumbing or landscaping — is simply asking if you can put a brochure in the neighbour's letter box. Easy, but effective. On the back of the brochure write a note saying something like: My team is working at such and such a house. If there's any problem with the noise, the parking, or the guys that are working there, please let me know. It's just a nice courtesy… and you get eyes on your brand.

On that point, you can also put a flyer or brochure in the neighbour's letter box offering a great sales promotion. The trick is you've got to make an offer that's enticing enough for them to act straightaway. For example, an offer of '10% off' is not enough… and a free audit of their plumbing isn't really all that crash hot either... but '$50 - $75 off' for new customers to fix a tap? That might do the trick!

Maybe an "irresistible offer" (one so good they can't say no to it!) from a car mechanic could be free wipers for every new customer. The wipers might be worth $30 – $50, but you're getting a new customer for LESS than the profit made on the first job. The real money is found when they bring their car back for future services!

Trial several offers to test the most effective for your business.

Don't overlook the obvious – signage. On your van, on your shirt, on your hat. Make sure wherever you (and your tradesmen) go, you're brand is clearly visible. Bang a big phone number up on the side of your van like we organised for Greater Western Electrical below.

27 Quick & Easy Ways To
Market Your Tradie Business

1. Call your dream customers!
2. Go to their business
3. Mail (Put something in the customers' neighbour's letter box every time)
4. Local newspaper advertising
5. Flyers/Brochures
6. Fridge Magnet
7. 'Leave behind your brand' in the cleaner's cupboard (like a painted stencil, tile, etc)
8. Business Card
9. Write them a Christmas card
10. Signage on the van
11. Signage on the shirt and hat
12. Sales promotion (create an "irresistible" offer)
13. Leave behind a business card at the local coffee shop
14. Stickers + Keyrings
15. Networking Functions (also get your name out there via other tradie owners)
16. Competitions
17. Referral System
18. Social Media/Facebook Ads (make sure you can get directly in touch with your DREAM customer though)
19. Website

20. Promo
21. Gifts for Dream Clients
22. Branded promotional products – stubbie holder, pens, note pad, mugs, toilet roll (great for a plumber!), light globe (great for a sparky!), safety hat (great for a chippy!), construction cones, drink bottle, Swiss knife
    `and confectionary
23. Discounts for bulk orders
24. Stay in touch – cards, emails, letters
25. Create a VIP card
26. Ask customers to buy from you again
27. Follow up & follow up again!

How To Set Up A Referral System

For smaller companies, great marketing is all about having a great referral system. When tradie owners say they get a lot of referrals, I ask them HOW they are getting those referrals and their response is usually, *"I don't know because they just come in. If they come, they come and if they don't, they don't."*

Even with just the most basic marketing in place, we need to take immediate action to get more referrals on purpose. We want a system set up that rewards customers who refer other people to our business.

I'm a huge advocate for writing up a referral system and having a prewritten script of what to say to entice customers to refer their friends, families and colleagues to you. I'm actually a huge advocate for writing a script at EVERY interaction you have with a customer to streamline the entire process, make your life easier, get better results and know your team is always presenting your company in the right way.

What's something you can do that would encourage a customer to give a referral?

Simply ASK for referrals! "Would you mind recommending me to your friends or neighbour if they have a need for my services?"

On many occasions, the neighbour will see you and your van and will then talk to the homeowner about you especially if they're needing a similar service done. At the end of the job, tell your customer you would appreciate it if they put in a good word for you. Of course, you can sweeten the deal by offering them a small gift in exchange, but sometimes just the art of asking is enough. If you have done a good job, most people are happy to refer others to you.

When To Ask For Referrals

WHEN	TO DO
Phone enquiring or quote stage	• Ask directly for a referral
On the job	• Ask directly for referral • Leave behind card, magnet, flyer, floor tile or stencil of logo and contact details
Invoice stage	• Ask for a referral at the bottom of the invoice
Follow up phone call	1 month later... • Ask directly for a referral • Send something to the customer (letter, email, gift)

Chapter Ten

INCREASING SALES
& Getting Better Work

Say the word 'sales' and tradie owners seem to freak out. Before you do that, know this: selling your service is vital if you want to stay in business over the long term. Obviously, you can't stay in business if you don't have any customers buying from you.

The often-overlooked thing with sales is that there IS a way to "sell" that's 100% genuine – yes, really: you do NOT (and should not) become a slimy or sleezy salesman – because by "sell" I simply mean making sure someone says 'yes' to working with you and not 'yes' to the guy around the corner who charges way more for his service and doesn't do as good a job.

At the end of the day, the definition of work is someone paying you to do something helpful for them. This section is making sure potential customers know how you can help them. Just because you're great at what you do, it doesn't mean other people automatically know this about you, so you have to showcase this.

Showing you're the right person for the job and increasing the likelihood that a potential customer will say 'yes' to working with you (and not someone else) is really what I mean by 'sales'. There's none of that "shark in suits" methodology here. It's about creating a great first impression, delighting your customers and setting up some systems so you can get on with the job of helping people out.

This chapter is all about mastering the sales side of your business without coming across as a douche bag or desperate.

My five top solutions are:

1. Be 100% Genuine
2. Have A Sales Process In Place
3. Capture Customer Testimonials
4. Showcase A Portfolio of Work
5. Create A Website

#1: Be 100% Genuine - You are not the type to pull the wool over someone's eyes so don't suddenly feel the need to become some master influencer or sales gun, just be yourself. Explain who you are, what your company does and how you can help. People like people who are themselves and we prefer to buy from people who are genuine. I would rather give my money to an upfront, decent bloke any day of the week than someone who has a perfected a sales pitch. Always be 100% genuine when dealing with potential customers.

#2: Have A Sales Process In Place One of the most powerful steps you can take that will leave a lasting impression on a potential customer is to give them a fast and polite response to their request, answer the phone or email quickly! This can happen automatically if you put a follow-up system in place. Once a quote is written, call or email the customer to make sure they've received it. The reason we always follow up is because they might not check their emails regularly, or your email might have ended up in their junk folder, or you might've accidently put in the wrong email address. Always double check that they've received it. While you're there, ask them when you can discuss this quote with them, and deal with any objections or questions they might have. This is absolute gold in terms of getting work!

Here's an example of a Sales Process to turn phone/ website enquiries into paying customers:

```
                    ┌─────────────────────────┐
                    │   Incoming Inquiry      │
                    └─────────────────────────┘
                                │
                                ▼
                    ┌─────────────────────────┐
                    │      5-10 Min Chat       │
                    │   Get full contact details │
                    │   for quote. Names, phone │
                    │   nos, email, job address, │
                    │        job details.       │
     Within 1 hour  └─────────────────────────┘
                                │
                                ▼
                    ┌─────────────────────────┐
                    │    Email Confirmation    │
     As booked      └─────────────────────────┘
                                │
                                ▼
                    ┌─────────────────────────┐
                    │       Meet Onsite        │
                    │     Ask for drawings     │
    1-2 days later  └─────────────────────────┘
                                │
                                ▼
                    ┌─────────────────────────┐
                    │       Email Quote        │
                    │     Also send Google     │
                    │     Reviews and/or       │
                    │       testimonials       │
     2 days later   └─────────────────────────┘
                                │
                                ▼
                    ┌─────────────────────────┐
                    │   Phone To Check If      │
                    │    Quote Received        │
     7 days later   └─────────────────────────┘
                                │
                                ▼
                    ┌─────────────────────────┐
                    │       Call To Close      │
                    │    Book in or handle     │
                    │        objections        │
                    └─────────────────────────┘
```

#2 Sales Process cont. As mentioned earlier, I'm a HUGE advocate for running a sales script whenever you speak with a customer. A sales script is a written dialogue of what to say to them at a specific point in time to help increase their likelihood of doing business with you. It can literally be a word-for-word script of what to say to them or can be a loose list of predetermined talking points, questions and overall conversation structure.

The idea behind it is not just to save you time and make sure you have a consistent message (which your team can say too!), it comes down to the fact that most people tend to ask the same questions, so you can be ahead of the game with what to say and can address some of their main problems and questions straight off the bat.

The real bonus is you can streamline the process, be much more confident with what you say and remove the annoying to-and-froing with time wasters. Obviously, be genuine with the scripts you come up with and tailor them to your business. Including testimonials or great reviews in your follow up scripts (and in an emails) can be very successful as potential customers are keen to know what working with you is really like from someone who's been there and done it.

Have a script for:

- 'Incoming Calls' – when someone calls to ask about your business
- 'Scheduling To Meet' – when someone is meeting you for the first time
- Onsite Measuring and talking to the customer
- 'Follow-Up' – after sending out a quote, after doing the job, after invoicing, etc

Example Sales Script: At The Start Of A Job

This is an example Sales Script between what an Electrician (James) might say to his client (Tracy) at the beginning of a new job. You would follow the same (or very similar) dialogue for all new jobs, and you would write down this script and give it to all your workers to use on site at each new job.

James: "Good morning/afternoon Tracey. I am James from Western Electrical I am here to look at/fix your "job requirement". James needs to be wearing company shirt/hat and importantly confirms the booking using the customers name.

Tracey – Hi James thank you for coming. Why don't you come in and I will show you the "problem"?

James: Great. You lead the way.

Things you need to mention are:

- Outline the job and agree.
- Make a statement around your company's Unique Selling Proposition (USP). Eg: "We are experts at doing this kind of work around Bacchus and Melton..." (More on USP in a later chapter)
- Make a statement or give flyer around your full range of services.
- Confirm if they will be there at the end of job and if it's OK to make payment then.
- Ask, "Since I am here, is there anything else you would like me to look at?" Wait for an answer, then suggest they walk around their house to test everything and let you know before you finish.
- Say that you will also look at the state of the switchboard to make sure it is safe. (Offer an over-and-above level of service, even if you would check all this anyway!)

At end of job:

- Check if they are happy with the job
- Check if they have found any other work for you
- Give Fridge magnet and place on fridge for them
- Show them the sticker in switchboard
- Tell them the outcome of the switchboard check. (The over-and-above offer)

- Ask for payment
- Ask, "Do you mind if you can give us a google review?" Send link via sms and help them do it.

#3: Capture Customer Testimonials What do most people do when they're considering using a company? They check out what other people have said about it! The very first thing people do when deciding if they want to work with you or not is to look at the reviews and testimonials from other customers.

When it comes to selling your trades service, there's no better person to do it for you than your own customers! We're all far more likely to believe what a customer has to say about a business than what the business does so you must capture as many great reviews from your existing customers as possible.

These can be written reviews or, even better, video testimonials where your customer leaves a review for your business on camera. While not every one of your customers will be comfortable or willing to do this, some will. This will be hugely beneficial for your business as you can use this testimonial in many different places. On your website, in follow up scripts, in brochures and flyers, on social media, in emails… you name it.

Your potential customers will also check out your Google Review ranking. After you finish a job, always ask your customer if they'd take 20 seconds out of their day to leave you a five-star review or a rating of their choice (most people will leave a high ranking if they're satisfied with the job. This way they know you're keen for real feedback, which they will appreciate even more and will further incentivise a higher ranking. To make this process super easy for them, you can send them a direct link to your company's Google review page – this is something you can automate by scheduling it out as a text message or email after every job is complete. This further highlights where a sales script is useful – you can literally use the same one over and over again:

Hi [Customer Name],
Thanks again for choosing [Company Name] – it was a pleasure working for you today. If you have a spare 20 seconds, would you mind leaving us a 5 star Google Review? Even if it's just a star rating – [link] Appreciate your valued business and look forward to working with you again in future.
Cheers,
[Your name]

#4: Showcase A Portfolio of Work This one is similar to the customer reviews, except you would showcase the work you have done for them. This way potential customers can get a visual on the type and quality of work you provide. You can also choose to showcase the work you really want to do or be more 'known for' as this will attract a customer who needs that particular job done.

When you (and your workers) are on the job site, take 'Before' and 'After' pictures EVERY time. Make sure this is a specific instruction you give out to your tradies. You can use these pictures on your website, social media (Instagram is a good one for these type of shots), and as a follow up script for potential customers who are keen to see what sort of work you do.

Start building and extending on a portfolio of work as soon as possible, and remember to add to it with EVERY job. Of course, you can hand select which ones you want to publish, but get into the habit of getting out your phone and taking a decent picture of the job site. *Before and after.* It'll take 2 seconds and is very much worth it – both from a sales sideand good for the guys on site to see the fruits of their efforts!

#5: Create A Website We live in the world of Google. If someone needs some trade work done, they're going to Google it. This means you MUST have a website. (If you're not on the internet, but your competitors are, you're in big trouble. You can build a simple website for free – or you can invest a small portion of cash to get someone to do it for you.

I would opt for someone else to roll it out for you as there are experts out there who can do it very quickly and make tweaks to it so that it's far more likely to be one of the first websites a customer will see when they run a Google search.

Obviously, there are many reasons why a website is extremely useful, but here's a few big ones:

- It works 24 hours a day... even when you've clocked off
- It makes your business look super professional
- You can showcase a portfolio of work and customer reviews
- You can book people in straight away (if you want)
- It cuts down the time wasters (they can get all the information online without wasting your time on the phone)
- Customers can find you more easily

- You can showcase who you are and what your company does so you can stand out from the competitors
- It's a brilliant marketing tool
- It saves you stacks of time and money

This way when you DO get new customer calls, it's normally from people who already have a fair idea of who you are and what your business does, so they are much more likely to work with you.

Again, you can get someone to build a website for you at a pretty reasonable rate, or you can bootstrap it and use a D.I.Y website-building platform.

These are usually free or inexpensive, though you might be required to pay for a domain name (an easy-to-remember 'www.' name like www.actioncoachgeelong.com.au) and a hosting fee. Some of these websites include: WordPress.org, GoDaddy.com, Squarespace.com, Wix.com or Strikingly.com. There are plenty of other ones out there to choose from – simply 'Google it' and you can see for yourself the power and knowledge in the World Wide Web!

Chapter Eleven

PROFITABILITY

How To Accelerate It

The key to turn your business into your personal wealth machine is to make sure the darn thing is PROFITABLE! Too many tradie owners I've worked with have no real clue 'Where all their money's going'… and a lot of this has to do with having lousy profit margins in place. They're undercharging, underestimating their cost of labour, miscalculating the time it takes to actually get the job done and have tradies on the job who simply aren't productive!

This doesn't just mean you miss out on good money; it actually means you are LOSING it… time and time again! I don't know about you, but I think that's a crying shame for all the hard effort you put in.

What do all tradie owners need to know to get their profitability sorted ASAP?

There are **FOUR** areas you need to master to improve profitability are:

1. **Pricing:** How much you should be charging for your services
2. **Real Cost of Labour:** How much your tradies are REALLY costing you (warning: most owners are shocked here)
3. **Billing Rules:** How much to charge for Billable Hours (and how to get your tradies to fill in their time sheets correctly so the rules stick)
4. **Productivity of Staff:** How to get the most out your employees while still keeping them happy (but working hard)!

While improving revenue and profit in business is the favourite subject of virtually every business owner out there, we need to look at these specific strategies that apply directly to trades businesses. Often this is where the wheels are falling off or, let's face it, aren't even screwed on to begin with!

Pricing
How Much You Should Be Charging For Your Services!

I met Tom about four years ago. He's a real smart guy. He started his plumbing business seven years ago as a mature 55-year-old plumber who went out on his own. His complaint was that he couldn't charge for all his time. He worked every night on his invoicing. He was also unhappy with how much he was earning. He was charging $80 an hour, which was low in the current market. He didn't know any better and needed an outsider to look at his numbers.

I had talked to Tom a few times over the last 4 years, but for whatever reason he didn't want to begin the business coaching process. Recently, he acknowledged this after I said, *"Tom, I think I've proven that by not working with me for four years, it has cost you about $150,000 because you haven't been focusing on improving revenue or profit."*

What did we tweak that was SO important and so overlooked? ... PRICING.

Tom adjusted his pricing and his solved the root of his problem. This is really common with people I work with. They presume that all purchase decisions are based on price and so they don't want to up their fees or, if they're busy, they see no urgency to change, despite the fact they're losing money with almost every job.

I understand that tenders are very much price-oriented, but for virtually all other jobs, there are a lot of other factors at play. In fact, about 80% of the buying decision is emotional. If we are quoting we must presume that there's a 80% chance that the reason for the job is emotional, so we need to reflect this in the way we present our quotes.

Maybe your customer is putting in a new decking in the backyard so they can be proud to show off their home when they have friends over. Maybe they're installing solar panels because they have an emotional connection to the environment. The new bath installation is because they saw one just like it in on The Block so they'll feel luxurious, nurtured AND cool while taking a bath.

People will pay more for what they value. When it comes to emotional decisions, people's logic brain goes out the window. In fact, most of your customers are making their decision on EMOTION, and then justifying it on logic. *"Oh, but we do really need the bath for the kids"*.

Before you think – "Yeah, but a blocked kitchen sink is a blocked kitchen sink..." it simply needs fixing. I agree with you but the main problem your customer has is that it's an absolute pain in the arse to go to fill up the kettle for your morning coffee and realise the tap's stuffed. I can assure you the emotion is driving the need to fix the tap ASAP.

In general, tradespeople are introverted and unoffensive people. You lot generally don't want to do a 'hard' sell, so the greatest opportunity to improve your business is through understanding and improving your pricing and sales. I'll walk you through a real life example of exactly what this looks like in a moment and I dare say you'll be shocked at some of the areas where you're not just "leaving money on the table", but also you're actually ripping yourself off! If you do any form of Unit pricing in your business, you'll need to be across this.

You also need to charge up your time. Plumbing maintenance contractors, for instance, might predict a job is small. Once they get to the site, they find more issues and they are there for several days. Some difficult customers might expect to pay you for time onsite only, so positioning the customer on how the job will run before you begin the work is crucial. Remember to make sure ALL your time is allocated the job and you are paid for it.

Without having a real focus on pricing, some owners are simply just too nervous to mark prices up. 10%

is simply not enough. Marking up materials by 10% is usually a zero-profit activity, along with all the paperwork that goes with it! Not to mention the left over, wastage, and pure loss. Tradespeople should be making a minimum of 20-30% on all materials, even if it's a big job because they're handling the money, taking the risk, and doing the warranty.

PRICING IN ACTION

How Brendon & Sue Fixed Their
Profitability Problem

Let's pick up where we left off with Brendon and Sue from Book One. Remember they needed $188,160 a year to fund their dream lifestyle and make sure they're well taken care of in retirement?
Remember they weren't sure if their electrical contracting business was making enough money… and this was BEFORE we even worked out how much they'd need?! (More than they thought.)
Clearly there was work that MUST be done in their business. What did we do to fix the problems and turn their dream into a reality?

Here's what we discovered:

We analysed their business as a whole and realised – oh no! – their profit margin is low. This explains why they don't think they're really earning that much… they aren't.

In fact, the business really wasn't making much money. We had no clue how much they should be earning. Neither of them are paid a wage they just take drawings out of the business when they need cash.

Reviewing their job management system (Aroflo) we could see that certain jobs weren't very profitable. Thankfully they had the foresight to use an online platform that replaces paperwork and manual processes. From what we could gather some of the builders' jobs made no gross profit at all! Housing rewires were looking pretty grim. They weren't making money... so there was a problem.

We had another (rather big!) problem... we weren't actually certain if the information in AroFlo was correct! If the information in the system wasn't correct, then we had no real clue what was going on.

It looked like the staff weren't using the time sheet applications properly. They weren't allocating all their hours to job and often they weren't allocating their time to the right job. To add to the headache, it also looked like they weren't updating the notes on the small jobs either – we couldn't see any parts or materials that were taken directly off the shelf in the workshop captured anywhere. This is a problem.

If there's no paper trail for wholesale costs, it makes everyone's life hard. Sue must still invoice for these items, but without a clear description or record of them, she doesn't know what to charge.

Things are missed. Things are guessed. Things are now difficult for the clients too.

As Sue doesn't know any details, there are invoices all over the shop for "Fixed electrical" with a rounded number – $5,000 seems to be the go to – as the total cost. This has many problems in itself, but when these problems affect the customer directly, it becomes a much bigger problem. Every customer in the history of customers wants an itemised receipt. They want to know what cost was associated with what. They want to know they're paying for the right service and for the right stuff in this case, they're likely underpaying. Every day seems to be a "lucky" day for customers. Not so lucky for Brendon and Sue though!!)

There's also details missing around billing rules. The guys are writing down "4 hours" to complete a job, but we have no idea if that includes the drive to the wholesaler. We just don't know. As Sue invoices a week after the job and calls the guys to ask of course, they can't remember. Now we have no idea if the total labour time has been captured correctly. To top it all off, we had no idea what the REAL cost of the labour is.

Brendon and Sue had a number in the system, but this number wasn't correct. It didn't capture the overheads for Sue's labour, for the wage she should be receiving but wasn't. Nor did it factor in Brendon's real worth to the business reflecting his time, skillset and business risk. If the latter's not there, you may as well just go out and get a job. This is all just on pricing. These issues are just on making sure we can price properly. We have barely even scratched the surface of what to improve in Brendon and Sue's business.

Here's how we fixed the pricing problem:

1. First, we worked out from the accounting package that they weren't earning enough. We knew this from gut feel, but now we had the proof.
2. This was then confirmed in the job management system (AroFlo). Now we knew with 100% certainty they aren't earning enough. You don't go into business to undercharge, be underpaid and barely profitable, people.
3. We started selecting better quality customers and jobs that were more profitable.We started

this process almost immediately. We made good money on underground power supply, so that was a keeper... and we culled the unprofitable jobs NOW. Goodbye housing rewires!

4. We set about confirming if what was in AroFlo was accurate. This was a very big job. We checked everything from timesheets, the info from the guys, invoicing... ALL of it!

5. We started training the guys on how to use the system CORRECTLY and update their timesheets directly in AroFlo .They'd been using separate timesheets, so there were errors all over the place. Not to mention they were paid from AroFlo anyway, so it made way more sense! Prior to this change, when it was time to do pays, Sue would always have to call the guys one by one to ask for their timesheets... literally every week, like clockwork. So she'd always have to work Wednesday nights just to chase up pays... but now she's got her time and night back!

6. We broke down the Unit Pricing for EVERYTHING – labour and materials. After chatting with Brendon and Sue, I realised the "standard rate" for almost everything was pretty much made up. There was no basis for unit pricing. For example: when I saw "Downlight" on an invoice, I asked him how he got to the

price of $120 and what was included in it.

"I dunno. $120 sounded about right. You've got the light globe, a cable and a couple of screws... just a tiny bit of labour. A hundred and twenty bucks should do it." I then asked him if he was presuming 2 metres for the cable, and if he knew the exact cost of labour based on how long it took to install this particular light fitting. *"I'm not sure on the exact cost, no. But yeah, about that for the cable. It varies from job to job, but it all pans out in the mix."* Well, no, it did not all pan out in the mix. Because Brendon was NOT making money! If he wasn't correctly charging for everything and ignoring that it really took 45 minutes of labour to install, he was practically giving his money away and working for free.

How did we work out the Unit Pricing?

We got VERY clear on what costs were involved for EVERY aspect of the job, and organised them into the table (pg 165). The category descriptions mean:

- **Description:** This lists the EXACT materials used for each the job (down to the size of the cable used).
- **Materials cost:** A list of all the materials included and their wholesale current cost.

- **Labour hours:** How much time it took to complete the job (this varies for each individual job so this number needed to be an ACCURATE reflection for each).
- **Labour rate/hr:** The REAL cost of labour per hour (not just how much you are paying your staff).
- **Labour cost total:** The total cost of labour based on the time it took to complete the job.
- Total cost ex GST: The total cost of materials and labours, excluding GST (and with no markup at this point).
- **Markup:** How much to add to the total cost of goods so you earn enough to cover the costs of doing business and create a profit – here we have chosen a markup of 1.35 because this covers overheads of the business, plus an acceptable profit for Brendon and Sue (this number will vary based on each individual business).
- **Sell price** ex GST: How much you should charge for the job, based on everything we've worked out (total cost + markup).
- **Current Cost**: How much you are currently charging for the job, so you can see a direct comparison between the Sell Price (what you should be charging, minus GST) and what you are currently charging.

Item No	Description	Details	Materials Cost EX GST	Labour Hrs	Labour Rate/Hr	Labour Cost Total	Total Cost EX GST	Markup	Sell Price EX GST	CURRENT COST
1	LIGHTING POINT	10M 1.5 CBL, Batten Holder, Led Globe, Clips, Labour	17.81	0.5	$99.00	$49.50	$67.31	1.35	$90.87	$44.00
2	DOWNLIGHT <3 MTRS	1.5 10M CBL, HPM D/L, 415 QC, Clips Labour	32.82	0.75	$99.00	$74.25	$107.07	1.35	$144.55	$104.50
3	STANDARD PENDANT	1.5XBL, Timber Noggin, Clips, Labour	10.03	1	$99.00	$99	$109.03	1.35	$147.19	$143.00
4	316 SS DOWNLIGHT	10M 1.5 CBL, Havitt Fitting, 413 QC, Clips, Labour	94.58	0.75	$99.00	$74.25	$166.83	1.35	$227.92	$121.00

Now, this wasn't an "overnight" task – Brendon and Sue had to put in a bit of effort in to compile all this information but it was probably one of the BEST uses of their time in the business ever.

This spreadsheet was filled with literally every job the business does, but here is a very small example of just four of the jobs they do in the business: As you can see above, the *downlight* I'd asked Brendon about should actually be priced at $227.92… and he was currently only charging $121 for it.

That's more than $100 out of pocket… for ONE light fitting. As I mentioned, this is only the tip of the iceberg of more than 100 items on Brendon and Sue's total job's pricing list. Even with just these four items, you can see the huge gaps between what they should be charging (the "Sell Price") and what they're currently charging (the "Current Cost"). For example: the 'Lighting Point' should be double the price! That's another $45 out of pocket for just one job for one client. And as you can imagine, there are often many of these little jobs per client so it all adds up. And it all adds up to a LOT! In fact, these particular four items are ALL under priced – and this small glimpse into Brendon and Sue's entire job list is pretty representative of the full picture!.

Sure, they might have a handful of jobs where they're pretty even on price (even less of these are overpriced), but mark my words: it does NOT all "pan out in the mix"! In almost every instance, they are undercharging. Look at the 'Standard Pendant' – it's pretty close to what the selling price should be, right? It's "just" $4.19 under, so there's no harm done it's not even five bucks, yeah? Wrong. $5 out for one product that you are consistently undercharging for is a lot.

That's like saying you'll shout your sparkies a takeaway coffee for every single light fitting they roll out – that $5 would quickly add up, right? All of a sudden, you're forking out $50 a day per guy on coffee… for no reason whatsoever… and you're going to consistently do this every single time he installs this particular light…on every job for years and years to come. You just wouldn't do that! So why do you think it's okay to give away "just" $5 on one of your products?! Here's the short answer: it's NOT okay. Every dollar adds up, and I'm telling you mate: YOU are the one copping the bill. No one else. So unless you like bleeding money, it's time to seriously look at your pricing structure!

7. We worked out how much the REAL cost of labour was! How did we work this out? Boy, was this one an eye-opener! Based on the table pg165, you can see that the hourly rate we have used for our labour rate is $99.00. This is representative of the most likely scenario for the purposes of our unit pricing model.

   We actually went one step further and worked out the REAL cost of labour for each employee! Word of warning: this is not the amount you pay your staff per hour… it's generally much higher than this and this is where a lot of tradie owners get in trouble with their pricing. They don't realise how much their employee is really costing them!

Real Cost of Labour
How Much Your Tradies Are Costing You!

Do you know exactly how much each employee in your business is costing you? Hint: it's NOT the hourly rate you are paying them! When it comes to identifying the real cost of labour, many business owners assume their tradies are costing them way less than they actually are. You must understand the true cost of an employee. It's not just their pay and benefits. There are many other expenses that you are literally footing the bill for that most owners are not even thinking about. All these additional costs, which I have listed below for you must be considered when you are evaluating how expensive each tradie is to your business.

This has a direct and immediate impact to what your pricing structure should look like as well as how you determine what sort of Return on Investment (ROI) you should be getting from each person in your team. There is absolutely a science to working this out (lots of number crunching) but understanding the real cost of labour is something every single owner on the planet should be doing... and doing immediately. I'll also run you through an example employee, so it makes more sense to you. Speak with a trusted business coach if you need extra guidance in this area.

Indeed, this has been a "penny dropping" moment for every single one of my clients over the last 11 years, and almost everyone is shocked when they first realise the TRUE hourly cost of each staff member. The cost that's not on the payroll but IS still coming out of your back pocket!

Here's a general rule of thumb, each employee is costing you about 40% more than you think!They're almost double the cost to your business You are paying for your employee even when they do absolutely nothing for your business.

Owners' costs DON'T just stop at the hourly rate for an employee. You also have heaps of other costs that go into employing someone to work with you. This is varied depending on whether they work full time or part time or casual in your business, but the extra costs to your business include:

Employment costs:
- annual leave
- paid sick leave
- paid public holidays
- superannuation
- payroll tax
- workcover

Other employment costs

- leave loading
- long service leave
- site allowances
- vehicle expenses
- other allowances

Overheads:

- rent, rates, utilities
- marketing
- accounting fees
- insurance
- shares/sales vehicles
- communications
- internal staff wages
- management wages
- all other costs

While most owners can understand the employment costs (but even so, often aren't factoring these into their real cost of labour), they're often completely ignoring the overhead costs and what it takes to 'keep the lights on' in their business... expenses that should be factored into the true pricing of your team.

Let's take a look at an example:

Jason is a full-time plumber. His pay rate is $35.50 per hour – this is the hourly rate he sees on his payslip, and this is normally what most owners think their employee is costing them. But this isn't the case. Jason's hourly rate is actually much higher than this. Here's why:

Jason works 38 hours/week for 48 weeks per year, which works out to be $64,772 as demonstrated.
35.50 x 38 x 48 = $64,772
(Hourly Rate x Hours Worked x Weeks Worked)

But the owner must also pay Jason for his four weeks' annual leave even though he won't work during this time and therefore, won't be making any money for you. So, you need to factor in this amount into the cost:

35.50 x 38 x 4 = $5,396
(Hourly Rate x Hours Worked X Annual Leave)

This additional amount needs to be added to the original number, which brings Jason's annual total up to $70,148.

This is commonly known as Jason's salary – but then you must pay superannuation on top of this, which is an additional 10%. And, don't forget, you've also got to pay him an extra 1.3% in Workcover too! We also have to pay him for the public holidays and sick days and any training days where he'll still be getting his money while not making you any. We have got to factor that in to make sure we recoup these losses somewhere:

Salary + Superannuation (10%) + Workcover (1.3%) + Other employment costs per period
$70,148 + $7,014.80 + 911.92 + $1,5000 = $79,574.72

This brings Jason's total direct costs to the business as **$79,574.72.** But like all things properly calculated, *there's more to factor in!*

Remember that we pay Jason his annual leave and his sick days and his public holidays and all that even though he won't be working and bringing in any income for us. This means that out of the 38 hours he is paid for each week for the year, only a certain percentage of these are "billable hours" Hours he is actually working on the tools to earn you money.

Hours Worked x Weeks In Year = Potential Billable Hours
38 x 52 = 1976

Potential Billable Hours – Non Billable Hours (the hours he will actually be away from work that we're still paying him for) = Total Billable Hours For The Year
1976 – 530.6 = 1445.40

This means that in the year Jason will work 1445.40 hours for you – this is the ACTUAL hours he will potentially be making you money.

Let's divide his total direct costs to the business by this hourly number to work out how much each billable hour is costing you.

$79,574.72 / 1445.40 = $55.05

Total Direct Cost / Total Billable Hours = Total Employment Cost Per Billable Hour

This means that when Jason is literally on the job, he is costing you $55.05 an hour... this is $19.55 MORE than his hourly rate! (Which, again, is $35.50).

But it gets even more expensive...

As the owner, you still need to keep the lights on when Jason is working for you, right? You've still got to pay for the rent, the electricity, the fuel, the factory, the cars and all that just for Jason to go do his job. In this business, for every potential man hour worked, the overhead is $28.58. So we need to add all that up too.

$55.05 + $28.58 = $88.63

Total Employment Cost Per Billable Hour + Over Head Per Hour = Total Cost Per Hour

Jason's REAL Cost to the business is $83.63 per hour.

It's a bit more than his hourly rate of $35.50, isn't it? You really need to make sure you're sending Jason to work on jobs that are costing you MORE than $83.60, don't you? Otherwise, you're losing money! If you're sending Jason to a job that's going to take an hour, you might want to make sure your call out rate is NOT $50 – because it's already costing you $33.63 to go to that job.

Even though Jason might only be doing a small job that takes 10 minutes, you need to keep in mind that you've got to pay Jason to get to the job, for the petrol for the car, for the time it takes to speak to the customer and introduce himself, to DO the actual job, finish up, pack up and then drive back to the factory. All of a sudden, an hour of Jason's time is gone but you've only been paid for a cheap 10-minute job. This is why you might look at sending your cheaper guy out to fix a leaking tap... because his cost to the business is much LESS than Jason. You need to look at your whole business model and pricing structure and determine if this type of job is even profitable to you.

This is why understanding the real cost of labour is so vitally important for every single trades business owner. You are footing the bill for so much more than your guys' hourly rate. You need to factor this in when working out how much their time is really costing you, and whether or not you are 'putting them to work' in the hours they are working and if you're pricing structure is set up to cover the full cost of labour.

BEST WAY TO QUICKLY CALCULATE COST OF LABOUR

Every client who works with me gets guided in my "Labour Cost Calculator" tool – it literally does the above process for you for EVERY staff member. All you really need to do is put in the current pay rate for each staff member, business overheads, and the rest is worked out in the background.

Because this tool is one of the best on the market (it's not as basic as some of the other generic "Cost of Labour" tools out there), I will need to walk you through it in case we do need to tweak anything else to suit your specific trades business (including your teams' qualifications). We can accurately tally this cost of labour and use this information to maximise the profitability in your business. Knowing the real cost of labour doesn't make you profitable, it is the starting point to work from, which requires direct business coaching.

Email me directly at hugh@actioncoachgeelong.com.au and mention this calculator to me and I'll walk you through it in our free strategy session together I don't normally do this for free... but I will if you mention this chapter.

Billing Rules

How Much To Charge For Billable Hours

With small companies doing a lot of little jobs, having an accurate measure of billable hours is key to charging the right amount for the work performed. Remember – "billable hours" is the time it takes to do the ACTUAL job. So, you need to set up a system that properly captures this length of time.

To make this super easy and as accurate as humanly possible, I have created a system for you called "Billing Rules". This is a little strategy I have used for many of my tradie clients to get them to properly train staff on what what's required (the "rules") for each job's time. I call it 'Billing Rules' as a way to help staff know what to put on their time sheets and when to raise a question about how to allocate time to a job.

Here's an example of some billing rules:

- Job is received – start the timer now
- Load the vehicle
- Drive there
- Do the job
- Drive back
- Unpack and clean up
- Do the invoice
- Submit the information – stop the timer now

You need to go through different job scenarios and clearly describe what's actually included in the job because if you're a business that relies on billing hours plus materials, you MUST be highly focused on making sure you're billing enough hours!

BILLING RULES - PLumber/Maintenance

* Start timer at 8am or job start
* Stop timer after vehicle fully packed, notes written, photo uploaded. Restart next job.
* End of day stop timer at end of job.
* Include supplier visits in job time.
* Time to pick up property keys to be included in the job.

Productivity

How To Get The Most Out Of Your Employees
While Still Keeping Them Happy

Productivity leads to good profitability there's no doubt about it! But how can you properly measure the productivity in your staff?

Here's what you need to know when it comes to maximising productivity from your tradies: the goal is to measure ACTUAL HOURS spent on a job compared to what's been quoted.

If you've miscalculated your quoting, it's not usually on materials... it's usually on labour hours.

One common issue with managing the productivity of your tradies is this; they aren't given a target time to complete the job! If they actually know the target, they're far more likely to aim to complete the job in this time. This is a huge opportunity for many businesses. Let employees know how many hours are allotted to finish a job.

For smaller jobs, it's essential you measure *Billable Hours Per Tradie* on either a daily or weekly basis. This can sometimes be a bit tricky, but a job management system can help out a lot if you use it properly. Make sure you train your staff on how to fill in their timesheets correctly so you know exactly how they have been spending their hours.

In general, for maintenance system businesses that do a lot of small jobs, staff need to be billing more than 80% of their time to jobs in order to be profitable. In my 11 years as a business coach, I've seen businesses running at less than 50% bill out ratio, which is just way too low. At least 80% of your tradies' time MUST be spent on billable hours.

Another strategy to improve productivity is to capture unbilled hours. Every business will have instances when their staff aren't 'on the tools' working directly on the job – for things like training, team meetings, etc.

What is acceptable to leave as unbilled or put down as workshop time? A great way to reduce this is to specify what is an acceptable amount of unbilled time for your employees. See below an example of what you think is acceptable amount of non-billable hours, and you can design your pricing system around this.

ALLOWABLE NON BILLED HRS

Employee	Hours NOT Billed
Tim	1.5hrs/day
Rob	1 hr/day
Blake	0.5hrs/twice per week
Luke	0.5hrs/twice per week

* Notify Tim if higher so that we can discuss how to be more efficient.

To recap, here are the three things you must do starting Monday to improve the productivity of your team:

- Measure actual hours spend on a job compared to what's quoted
- Measure Billable Hours Per Tradie
- Capture Unbilled Hour

Make sure you tighten these so that you are maximising your tradies' output at every stage. Obviously, your team is human and you want them to be enjoying their employment with you, but it's important you monitor their progress in terms of their dollar-producing output (at the end of the day, this is what 'keeps the lights on)

You can offer incentives to keep them focused on the task at hand (these really do work); however, it's more so important to set the expectation that they are there to get the job done as quickly and effectively as possible (without compromising on quality). So set the expectation, monitor and tweak accordingly.

Chapter Twelve

YOUR TEAM

How To Create A Loyal & Hardworking Team

There's no doubt about it: a great team means great results for your business. Everyone knows that a champion footy team is made up of star players… but star players don't win games on their own, do they? It takes the team to win, and it means every individual player needs to pull their own weight. Likewise, if you've got a whole bunch of players who aren't performing as great as they could be, or they're simply not capable of stepping up to the plate, how can you expect them to play at the top level.

The same is true for business. Sustainable success is always underpinned by the quality and execution of your team. Unless you want to do the entire job on your own (which you can't and shouldn't), you need to be able to rely on other people who will support you, do a ripper job, take care of your clients and, ultimately, work well with one another so you don't need to stress about what they're up to when you're not there – you trust them to get the job done.

Obviously, having a bunch of hard workers is an awesome start – but having a great team that work together, actually falls more on YOU (the business owner) than you think.

Picture this: the guys are rocking up to work late, and instead of going straight to the tools like they should be doing, they're cleaning the coke cans out of their car, they're asking the other guys, "Who's up for Maccas?!" or they're dragging their feet, maybe having a smoke or finishing up a personal call…

They've fronted up to work, but they're not READY to work – they're dicking around and doing God knows what on your watch. Then they're knocking off early, unloading the tools like time doesn't matter, and dawdling through jobs left, right and centre. *Why is this happening!?*

Answer: You have a problem with team culture. One bloke started being lazy and now they all are. Or everyone's seems to be doing whatever they want, whenever they want – they're not really listening; they are half-arsing jobs, and they don't seem to have any respect for you or your company.

Team culture is made up of the values, beliefs, attitudes and behaviours shared by a team of employees... so if you've got a bunch of staff members doing the wrong thing or not acting or thinking in a way that you'd like them to be behaving and thinking... it's on you.

This is where you need to knuckle down and actively think about your team culture and how to maximise everyone's effort and attitude.

There are Five Keys to unlock a winning team and as a business owner you want to jump on these five critical things quick smart. If you don't *course correct* bad attitudes or behaviour that's happening in your company you will find yourself in a position where your team is running YOU.... and you will have balls dropping all over the place, unhappy clients and a sea of stress all falling back on your shoulders.

The real gift of knowing how to create a winning trades team isn't just about avoiding the unpleasant stuff. The real secret of having an A-grade team of capable, confident and loyal workers is the difference between being a Wealthy Tradie and a poor one. Your people are not only the ones dealing directly with your clients (that is, the people who pay you) but also, they're the ones who will continue working so that you won't have to. They will keep you profitable, in business and – the big one – will keep your reputation in good nick so you can run your business like a well-oiled machine. It pays to put effort into getting the right people into your business, maximising their efforts, and making sure they stick around!

The Five Keys to Unlock A Winning Team:

- » **KEY #1:** Set The Rules of The Game
- » **KEY #2:** Run Regular Toolbox Meetings
- » **KEY #3:** Performance Appraisal With All Staff
- » **KEY #4:** Hire The Best Tradies
- » **KEY #5:** Get The Most From Your Apprentices

I'll work you through how to sharpen each key below.

KEY #1: Set The Rules Of The Game: The best way to create a great team culture is to make sure everyone is playing by the same rules. This where the Rules Of The Game come in – these are the standards in your company. Here's a little-known fact for you: the standards in your company are there even if you haven't actively set them! That's right. Your team will start to learn from one another about what's acceptable and what isn't so you must make sure YOU are the one setting the ground rules for what's okay and what's not okay in your own business. You will always *"get what you tolerate"*, so you need to transform your unwritten rules into written ones.

Another way I like to think about the Rules of The Game is "The Way We Do Things" – that is *"This is the way we do things around here."* It's a list of rules about how you want your employees to behave and what your daily expectations are. Including start and end times (eg. start time means have the toolbelt on and be ready to work at 7am). When and how they can use their personal phone (emergencies are okay; long conversations with mates are not) and how they conduct themselves on site (clean the worksite before you leave, etc).

The idea isn't to be a tyrant; it's to set some boundaries so they know how they should behave at work and when to draw the line. You wouldd show this rules list to every employee from Day 1 so they have a clear set of rules to follow and have no excuses about not knowing your expectations. This makes life much easier for you both. No one likes finding out too late that you don't like things done a certain way. This is true for both the owner and employee. It gets everything out in the open, everyone on the same page, and stops anyone from being grumpy without openly expressing what's going on. You can make this the last one of your rules. *Let me know when something is bothering you and we can solve the problem together.*

Make sure you involve your staff and ask them to contribute. It helps get their buy-in so they are more likely to do what you want them to.

How to create your Rules of the Game:

1. During a toolbox meeting, give all staff a copy of this template, and discuss each point as a group
2. Tweak the rules to suit YOUR business – don't include something that isn't relevant, and add more rules if you need
3. Everyone participates, including the owner
4. Once you have finalised your rules as a group, print and give to each staff member.
5. Put recurring reminder in diary for 1st Friday/ Monday of the month (or similar), and revisit the rules as a group, as time goes on you may need to add more rules, or change existing ones if no longer suitable.

Rules of The Game – Example

1. **Work Hours** - Minimum 7:00am to 3:00pm Monday to Friday. Inform XXManagerXX if you are leaving your job earlier or later than start and finish times above. i.e., to go to the dentist, doctor etc. Be Punctual! If planning to be off work please give XXManagerXX one weeks' notice in advance. Please arrive on site by 6:55am.

2. **Tea break and lunch break** – 20min Tea Break in the morning and 30mins lunch at XX. Driving to buy lunch is included in lunchtime.

3. **Phone use** - Personal phone calls during working hours are expected to be very short (i.e. <2mins) and only if urgent. Social media, messaging, and organising afterwork activities to be done during breaks.

4. **Job management system:**

   a.   Enter work times daily in AroFlo at the job. Alternately you can use the start/finish timer function in AroFlo, but must remember to clock off.

   b.   Start time and finishing times to be correct. Make sure times are correct when moving from job to job. Any discrepancy in timesheets will be seen as misconduct.

5. Worksite:

a.   At the end of the day clean your work site. This includes your lunch rubbish.

b.   Materials no longer required onsite are to be returned to supplier for credit. Useable and nonreturnable items/offcuts to be returned to shed.

c.   All materials purchased for a job must have an order number. Do not throw out fittings, pipe, screws, clips, scrap, etc. when cleaning vans – sort through before dumping in bin. Do not leave scrap copper onsite; spend the extra 10 minutes taking it from site. Place in shed scrap bin.

d.   Wear protective safety boots at all times

6. Tools:

a.   If wanting to purchase tools/materials on account for yourself you must ask XXManagerXX first. Order number is required. We are happy for you to be able to buy materials at commercial rates.

b.   Any broken tools need to be reported and handed to XXManagerXX for replacement. Do not misuse company tools. They are to be cleaned after use if needed.

7. Vehicles:

a.   Respect company vehicles and report any damage immediately. This includes cleaning any rubbish out and unpacking leftover materials at the end of the day.

b. You must pay for any fines you get while using the company vehicle.

c. If doing your own jobs, you're welcome to use utes but please advise if you are travelling over 25km round trip.

d. Company vehicles are to be cleaned weekly in own time. Typically, every week/fortnight or when dirty.

8. **Workshop:** Workshop/shed area to be kept tidy. Tools and materials to be shelved at the end of every week.

9. **Smoking:** - Not during working time. If smoking during your break please smoke outside.

10. No alcohol or drug use – Instant dismissal.

11. ALWAYS wear your uniforms (supplied) and be presentable. We want all our customers to look at us as very professional.

12. Respect your team mates, their tools, and their workmanship.

13. If for any reason you are unhappy with work, the people you work with, the way jobs are run or managed, be sure to raise it with XXManagerXX. There is no point in stewing on an issue. The aim is to have a great team.

ACTION ITEM

- Create your own Rules of The Game!
- To get the printable PDF copy of the above rules for free, head to
  www.wealthytradie.com.au/freebies

READ ON....

KEY #2: Run Regular Toolbox Meetings. Mate, if there's one thing I can stress, it's this: you've got to run a REGULAR team meeting with your guys. Yes, I'm talking about having a "toolbox meeting" each and every week. Too many tradie owners seem to skip this or think it's not great use of their time, but having worked with hundreds of business owners over the years, I can assure you it's a vital use of your time. This gets all the guys on the same page, keeps you on track to hitting your key business goals and helps build good team energy. Keep the meetings short and sharp so you're not wasting anyone's time, and come to the table with an agenda to talk through.

You can choose just one or two key things to focus on or you can run a meeting similar to what I've mentioned below. (I run something very similar for my own team!) You might notice that the meeting begins by engaging the entire team, then shifts to measuring progress and accountability, and closes with future action steps and encouragement.

How To Create Your Toolbox Meeting

1. Have a different person "run" each meeting (with the help of the example sheet)
2. Everyone must come prepared

3. Everyone participates, including the owner
4. Keep to time
5. Put recurring reminder in diary for 1st Friday/ Monday of the month (or similar)

Toolbox Meeting – Example

1. WIFLE ("What I Feel Like Expressing") – 4 mins. Each team member gets 15-30 seconds to say what's on their mind, without interruption. It can be work or home related (they can simply say what they did on the weekend). Only 1 person speaks at once. You might learn something fun about them, or at least know where their head's at.
2. Recent Wins (things going well) – 5 mins. Think of 1 or 2 specific wins each. Can be individual or team.
3. Learning (shared for the benefit of others learning)
4. Owner Update on Company Goals – Monthly, 2 – 5 mins
5. Discuss "The Rules of the Game" (Culture Statement) – Monthly, 10 mins. Each person chooses 1 or 2 from the Culture statement and discusses where and when they applied it. (Must choose a different one each time)
6. Updates on actions from previous meeting

7. Operations -Weekly/fortnightly/monthly

   a. Upcoming jobs

   b. Feedback from clients (Good & Bad)

   c. Current jobs – stages/timings etc important to get right or done immediately.

   d. Issues or compliments with Timesheets or time spent on jobs

   e. Is there anything we can do better as a team with job management and communication

   f. Quality of workmanship discussion

   g. Productivity – Is there anything we can do to be more efficient?

   h. Has anyone been asked to do further work from client or other person?

   i. What has been done to encourage referrals? Update on how many the business has received.

   j. Vehicles – condition or maintenance

   k. Holiday planning

   l. Do we need to recruit anyone? Apprentice? Fully qualified?

   m. Safety – reinforce common safety practice in your industry.

8. Individual actions for the week/month (Each person to verbally state)

9. Meeting Close Out – make statement of optimism, encouragement, or praise

ACTION ITEM

- Put recurring reminder in diary for the 1st Monday of every week (or similar) to run your Toolbox meeting
- Get the FREE printable Toolbox Meeting sheet to print out so your team knows what you'll be covering each week here: www.wealthytradie.com.au/freebies

READ ON....

KEY #3: Do A Performance Appraisal With All Staff

In order to get the most from each member of your team and make sure you're both having fun while heading in the same direction, it's a good idea to do what's called a "Performance Appraisal" for each of your team members.

A Performance Appraisal assesses the job performance and contribution of an employee – basically, the two of you get together and discuss how things are going, review progress of the employee and if there's anything that can be improved in the work environment to maximise performance and enjoyability of the work.

It's a chance for you to sit down together without distractions every 6 – 12 months to keep your employee on track, give them an opportunity to air anything with you and reward high-achieving effort.

Before this 1:1 meeting, the two of you would take a moment to individually think about the employee's performance and fill out a form that assesses their KPIs (Key Performance Indicators – these are targets that measure progress and company success). After the meeting you would both sign off on the final copy and attach it to the employee job file so everyone is accountable to what was discussed and there's a record to refer back to when you have your next Performance Appraisal.

There are a few options of what you might include in this appraisal, but below are a few examples I've found particularly useful for my tradie clients over the years. (If you want the full printable version for free, please head to **www.wealthytradie.com.au/ freebies** to download it. It includes a section for you both to sign as well as some other useful information to cover during the Performance Appraisal meeting.)

Key Performance Indicators

Indicate whether the Key Performance Indicator is meet:

Key Performance Indicators	Achieved?
1. All hours and materials entered into (Job Management System) before leaving the work site.	Yes / No
2. Labour utilisation above 92%	Yes / No
3. Vehicle checklist completed on time	Yes / No
4. XYZ Tradesmen uniform worn at all times	Yes / No
5. No more than 2 call backs per month	Yes / No
6. Complete trades Inspection Checklist for appropriate jobs	Yes / No

Responsibilities

Indicate the level of achievement on the following responsibilities

KEY: 1 = Never | 2 = Seldom | 3 = Sometimes | 4 = Mostly | 5 = Always

Responsibilities	1	2	3	4	5
1. All credits are accounted for and photo of packing slip is entered into 'Supplier Documents' under the correct job number.	○	○	○	○	○
2. Feedback from clients indicates client satisfaction.	○	○	○	○	○
3. All broken/damaged equipment is reported immediately to your manager. (Make a record of this on the whiteboard in the workshop.)	○	○	○	○	○
4. Clear all rubbish from jobs and dispose of correctly. Cardboard flattened into the cardboard bin and recycling done.	○	○	○	○	○
5. All work carried out in the expected timeframe as per the 'Schedule' in (Job Management System).	○	○	○	○	○
6. Keep work vehicle clean and in working order, checking oil, water and tyre pressure every Monday morning and topped up as required.	○	○	○	○	○
7. Create variations in (Job Management System) ensuring time and materials go to the appropriate job number. Noting if subcontractor used or any other relevant information.	○	○	○	○	○
8. Work site is safe at all times, according to OHS regulations and XYZ Trades Health and Safety Policies.	○	○	○	○	○
9. Complete Quality Assurance checklist for jobs as requested and appropriate.	○	○	○	○	○
10. Upholds XYZ Trades Company Values	○	○	○	○	○

Discussion Points

- Since our last discussion, what have you done well?
- What could you have done better?
- Knowing what you know now, what would you do differently next time to improve your contribution to the team and to enjoy your work more?
- Do you have any goals (work or personal) that we can help you achieve?

- Is there any training you would like to have (or manager thinks would be beneficial)?
- Are there any other issues you'd like to discuss? For example, frustrations, suggestions to improve the business, feedback you'd like to give or anything else that is important to you?

ACTION ITEM

- Book in your Performance Appraisals for each team member now!
- To get the FREE printable Performance Appraisal sheet to fill out, head to **www.wealthytradie.com.au/freebies**

READ ON....

KEY #4: Hire The Best Tradies: There's no doubt about it one of the most challenging areas tradie owners face is recruiting great staff. You already understand that having a great team will massively contribute to the success of your business but why is it so bloody hard to find the good blokes who are hungry to work?

The real secret to finding (and keeping) the best tradies — and indeed the best staff across the board, whether it's your tradies on the tools or your A-graders in the office is attracting the right people from the get go! Your recruitment process is absolutely vital in order to attract the right people to your business. This will save you both time and energy so you can focus on business growth.

Here are my Top Five Tips to hire the best tradies:

Tip #1 – Make Your Business Attractive

From an outsider looking in, how attractive is your business to work for? Attracting great staff in a competitive environment always comes down to how great you come across as their new employer. It's the old adage of "What looks good is good" but it comes down to more than that too. To snare the right talent you also have to be a good employer!

It's not enough just to look good, you have to offer attractive incentives so the best tradies are drawn to your business and the ones you already have stick around.

Your employees need to know that they'll enjoy working for you and that they are going to be genuinely respected. Nowhere is this more immediately recognised than from how a company respects itself – and this is often revealed from first impressions.

How to determine if your business is attractive to staff and future employees:

- Do you stand out compared to other trade businesses in your area?
- How high are your standards of operation and service?
- Do you look after staff and value their input?
- Does your business look like a great business? Ie branding, signage, websites, social media.
- Do you have great customers and secure ongoing work? (The word gets around!)
- Do you fully understand what attracts great employees such pay rates, flexible time off, tool allowance, phones, leadership responsibilities or future opportunities?

- Ask your existing staff WHY they like working for your business and who they know who might also be interested in working for you.

Tip #2 – Clarify Your Expectations

When writing job descriptions, you need to clearly describe your expectations as an employer in order to weed out unsuitable applicants to your business. This is key to productive employees both on the tools and in the office.

Job Descriptions: What to keep in mind:

- Your job description should not only include the skills and experience you are looking for, but also the Key Performance Indicators (KPIs) of the role. KPIs measure the performance of the individual, so you need to outline how you expect your employees to perform (based on what criteria) and how they can expect to be monitored and reviewed over time.

- You need to include everything in your employment contracts so employees have a clear understanding of your expectations.

- In the interview (and in all your interactions with staff), come from a position of clarity Be clear on what your business does, how you look after your customers and what you expect from your team. This will benefit everyone in your business and will mean you can confidently tackle performance issues if they arise.

Tip #3 – Systemise Your Recruiting

Having a hiring process saves you time and reduces the risk of employing the wrong person for any role within your business. Questions to ask yourself:

- Do you have a recruitment system with a flowchart, steps and templates so that someone else in your office could run this process for you... and you only step in when you are face-to-face with candidates? If run well, the employment process should take less than 4 hrs of your time.

- Do you have a questionnaire to find out about their background and motivation to join your company? This has a double benefit of helping you ask them more suitable questions and also forcing the candidate to elaborate on why they would be a good fit for your company.

- Do you include staff in the process? At the end of the day, your staff will be working with future employees and they will train them in many of the company processes, so you want to make sure they are onboard the process and can offer guidance on the right candidate that you simply don't see.

Tip #4 – Advertise The Job Properly

It should go without saying, but I'm going to say it so it sticks: the job ad needs to be decent in order to attract decent people.

I understand that writing a compelling job advertisement is tough if you haven't had much experience with enticing copywriting. Bounce around ideas with your business coach, or ask your best staff what words and phrases would interest them, or take a look at some of your competitors' ads, or — if you're really stuck — get help from a professional recruitment agency.

How to create a great job ad:

- The most important start to any kind of job advertising is a compelling headline. A headline draws interested tradies to your advert so it's vital it stands out immediately.

Your headline needs to include issues that tradies find important like great pay, challenging work, solid team and so on.

- Remember when hiring new staff, attitude is everything — so you need to list the personal attributes to reflect this. Tradies will be attracted to your business if they feel they share the same values as the company.

- List the important benefits of working for your company and use technology such as video to give a real insight into who you are, what your work culture is like and your standard of operation.

- To save time and unnecessary phone calls, make sure you explain the application process in a preprepared email when anyone makes an inquiry.

Tip #5 – Advertise The Job Everywhere

The more eyes on your job ad, the better! To get your new job position seen by as many tradies as possible, it pays to get it out in as many places as possible! The more places you advertise, the bigger the pool of talent you can talk with, which means you can be more selective with hiring. Here are some quick tips:

- Advertise your job on multiple platforms including Facebook, LinkedIn, Seek and Indeed.

- Ask clients, current staff and your existing database of suppliers. Also use local newspapers and vehicle signage, as well as giving tradies the opportunity to apply for the role on your website.

- You could even use a $1,000 referral fee as an incentive! (FYI – This should demonstrate how valuable a great team member is to your business – you'll well and truly make the investment back… just make sure the new member sticks around!)

KEY #5: Get The Most From Your Apprentices

Back when I ran an industrial refrigeration business, I used to see apprentices just standing around on the job doing not much. They might've been looking over the senior bloke's shoulder, watching him work but often they were just standing there, twiddling their thumbs.

It used to drive me mad! Obviously, we all need to learn and of course they need to be looking over the other guys' shoulder from time to time, but I used to think, I'm paying this apprentice, I want him to be doing something.

I understand that one of the best things you can do to get the most out of everyone in your team is to make sure your apprentices are actually working. You win, he wins (everyone learns the most through doing), and – the big one – the job that's meant to be done, gets done.

To get the most out of your apprentices, try splitting the job into key activities so they always know what to prioritise and what to do when they find themselves 'standing around' waiting for someone to tell them what to do.

Split Tasks Into A & B Activities

'A' Activities – these are 'on the job' activities. That is, this is the billable stuff that gets you paid. You or your senior tradie would tell your apprentice what he is responsible for to complete the job. Ideally, you would have a discussion about this in the ute on the way to the job, so your apprentice knows what to expect once you arrive on site. (I'll run you through an example to demonstrate this below.)

'B' Activities – this is the lower-level default activity. That is, the "I don't know what the A activity is right now so I'm going to do the B stuff." You or your senior tradie would help your apprentice build a list of all these activities so he always knows what to do when the most pressing stuff is done or can't be done by him.

For example, let's say an Electrician and his apprentice are going to install a split system in someone's house:

On the way there, the key tradie should be telling the apprentice what to expect when they arrive on site and what tasks they'll be immediately responsible for. The tradie has already been to the site to do the quote, so he already knows there's a head unit and an outdoor unit and whatever else going on. He knows what side of the house it's on too, so during this conversation in the car he can point the younger bloke in the right direction.

When they arrive on site, the key tradesman will go out and survey the site or talk to the owner or builder, and so the 'A' Activity for the apprentice is very easy and obvious, right? He knows everything's got to come out of the ute, and he can be doing this while the key qualified tradie is busy elsewhere.

Instead of him standing around checking Service Mate and looking at drawings trying to understand what's going on – he's already been pre-prepared. He knows exactly what's needed and where to take it The head unit comes out of the ute, the compressor, the vac pump, gauges, copper, capping… all that stuff… and that's his main job. His *A Activity* is to get everything that's needed off the ute and organised and ready for the main tradie.

The *'B' Activities* include when they're back at the workshop the apprentice unloads the ute, puts the fittings away, puts the coke cans in the bin, and all that. Again, you or your head tradie would take him for a walk and help him write out his list so he always knows what's going on and doesn't have to stand around waiting for direction all the time.

A common complaint a lot of tradie owners have is this; they bring on a new employee and this person's absolutely great to start off with... but then they go downhill. Suddenly your great employee is no good. What happened?

The secret to make sure your new employees start off great and stay great comes with a big pill to swallow for most tradie owners: the issue has to do with you! I know, I've been there and it's not the most comfortable truth to hear. How you onboard new members of your team and how you manage the culture of your business has a massive impact on how great new employees stay. Given they started off great, you know that this capability is already in them you just have to make sure they stay that way. The even better news is there are 3 Hacks to make sure every new employee stays an A-Grader!

3 Hacks To Keep A New Employee On Track

HACK #1: *Measure Key Performance Indicators (KPIs)*

Organise a meeting, sit them down and go through line by line all their KPIs and the expectations you have of them in the role; especially what you expect in the first three or six months. Spend 2 – 3 minutes on every single line and get them to sign it off so they're really clear on what they're expectations are. This way they can't say, "Well, no one told me that…" or learn the wrong thing from someone else. Plus, they'll love the process – they get the comfort of knowing what to expect and will have the reassurance that once they hit their 3-month probation, they'll be flying through.

HACK #2: *Create A Culture Statement*

Create a paragraph or a couple of sentences about what your company does and what it stand for so every employee knows what the working environment is like and are motivated to do a great job. Better yet, list 8 – 12 things your company lives by (this is like the Rules of The Game) that includes work start and end times, whether you can use our mobile phone on site and how to treat company vehicles so there's no confusion about your culture.

HACK #3: Unlock The Power of The "One, Four, Eleven" System

This one is a ripper tip for all business owners out there, and I use it for my new employees too. Basically, you sit down in week one, week four and week eleven to discuss how the employee is travelling. They get a chance to say how they're going and you get a chance to say how you think they are going. Ask if there's anything you can do to help you improve the way they perform and make them an even better employee for the business. It's a great opportunity for you both to hear each other's feedback, nip any issues in the bud and create an environment that has the owner and employee working from the same page.

Chapter Thirteen

REVIEW

Review, "Rinse & Repeat"... or Pivot!

Now that you're a decisive and assertive business owner who has taken action to turn your business into your very own wealth generator it's time to take a step back and look at what's been achieved and track your progress against your initial plan.

Strangely, this review step often gets ditched or quickly forgotten about. Too many owners think they don't need to monitor and measure their progress, and that's simply not the case. Just like you'd go to the doctors for a regular health visit, the same is true when it comes to REVIEWING your goals, plan and performance. You have to have conduct a regular check-up!

Of course, you can choose to wait until you're sick, have a broken back, or on your death bed to visit your doctor, but that's a bit of a fool's quest. Prevention is always better than a cure, and when it comes to business and personal wealth success, what gets MEASURED always gets done. If you want the health of your business (and the livelihood of you and your family) to remain in good working order, I strongly suggest checking in on its vital organs to make sure they're still ticking away and functioning as they should be!

Congratulations! You've made it to final step in my proven system where we review how everything is performing! This includes checking in with your personal and business goals and ticking them off or creating new ones, tracking your wealth progress to see how much money you have created for your dream lifestyle, tweaking your budget, assessing the financial metrics in your business, and, finally, monitoring and refining your business action steps.

This process doesn't need to take a bucket load of time but you do need to carve out a bit of time in your diary to make sure it happens. Some of the review process takes less than five minutes and you only need to do it once a year, and other parts of the process need to be looked at more regularly and take a little bit longer to properly evaluate – so in this section I am going to walk you through WHEN and HOW you should be conducting your reviews.

This information will let you know if you should stick to what you're doing ("rinse and repeat" the process) because it's working for you, or if you need to make a change and pivot so that you're more productive, profitable and, ultimately, on the road to funding your dream lifestyle where you can retire wealthy while still having a tonne of fun along the way.

In terms of my proven system to build wealth through your trades business, this is where you currently sit:

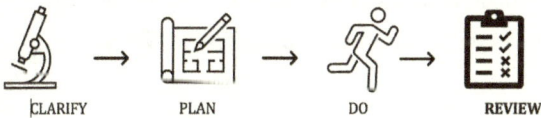

| CLARIFY | PLAN | DO | REVIEW |

In this section you'll learn:

1. WHAT to review to ensure your ongoing financial success
2. WHEN to conduct your reviews so you remain ahead of the game without doing any unnecessary work
3. HOW to run each review as quickly and efficiently as possible!

How To Quickly & Easily Master
The Review Rhythm

Ensuring your ongoing success always comes down to conducting a proper review on how you're performing. You want to know if this performance is in line with your Big Picture Plan. If it is... happy days! If not... it's time to pivot or make some tweaks to how you're running things.

To be super clear, chances are your big picture plan probably has a personal element to it. Such as buying a holiday home or having more time off. I go through this thoroughly in book one which you can obtain from **www.wealthytradie.com.au** . You can also download the free tools mentioned here: **www.wealthytradie.com.au/freestuff**

The aim of the game for The Wealthy Tradie is to get his business funding his personal wealth (financial, health, relationships, energy, time) – so you need to make sure you're checking in that this is actually happening for you! We don't want you slipping back into bad habits, and we also don't want you to be wasting your time with things that aren't actually giving you the best return on investment and serving your ultimate dreams.

We've obviously covered a lot of ground when it comes to both personal wealth and business success, so you'll find a few review steps for each stage.

Let's get into the timelines to review each activity.

W.I.S.H List

WHAT To Review:
Review your "What I Should Have" (W.I.S.H) List that we created at the very start of this process. You want to check in and tick off all the dreams you've turned into reality! You'll probably notice the momentum has lit a fire in your belly so you fully realise how much more cool stuff you can achieve if you put your mind towards it! Honestly, when I started this process myself, I couldn't believe how many of my own dreams I ticked off in my very first year – you might have a similar experience too and when this happens you can't help but want to add more dreams and experiences to your list! So, tick off those Big Dreams and add more if you feel so inspired!

WHEN To review:
At least twice a year (and the more often the better).

HOW To Review:

Simply check in with your W.I.S.H List!

You can download a new PDF Document here:

www.wealthytradie.com.au/freestuff

WHAT To Review:

This one is super exciting! Update The Wealth Tracker to reflect any changes in value to the assets you own. (Remember these assets are things like your house, car, business value, etc) – you will be pleasantly surprised how much your assets have GROWN in value without you having to do anything! (Yes, your house tends to go up in value while you're quietly chipping away at life!) Of course, you may notice that certain things have decreased in value... in this case, you'd want to ask yourself if it's time to let these particular assets go or if it's just a "wait and see" period. Of course certain things like cars and caravans often decrease in value over time (they're 'depreciating' assets).

WHEN To review:

Review every 6 months.

It's my preference to conduct a review every 3 months because I do think quarterly is best, but at a MINIMUM you must check this every 6 months!

It'll probably only take you ten minutes or so and I guarantee that you'll be absolutely chuffed when you see the uptick in your Nett Worth! That alone is worth the tiny investment of time. Go ahead and see for yourself!

HOW To Review:
Simply update your free The Wealth Tracker (TWT) tool – it will have remembered all of your information from last time, so this step simply involves looking up the new value of your assets and liabilities and putting them in.

If you can't remember, here's the links again:

- Home and all property – go to www.realestate. com.au or look at recent sales
- Cars – go to www.carssales.com.au
- Boats – www.boatsales.com.au
- Motorbikes – www.bikesales.com.au
- Superannuation – get in touch with your personal superfund
- Cash balances – your bank account/s
- Business value – see the next chapter for step-by-step instructions.
- Home & Investment Loans – check your statements or go to your bank branch
- Credit Card – check your credit card statements

- Personal Loans – check your loan statements or go to your bank branch
- Car Loans – check with your car loan provider or got to your bank branch

If for whatever reason, you need to access the FREE TOOL again, head here: www.wealthytradie.com.au/freestuff

Goals

WHAT To Review:

Your Personal AND Business Goals – tick off the ones you have completed and take some inspiration from your W.I.S.H list to prioritise some new ones.

WHEN To review:

Review at least monthly.

HOW To Review:

Check in with your own goals sheet or simply check in with your business coach to see how your BUSINESS goals are going… and if these are getting you on track to your PERSONAL goals. What can happen here is a tradie gets excited about working ON his business but still gets caught up in overworking, which goes against his personal goal of spending time at home with his family or taking that holiday he's always wanted to go on. The idea here is to make sure that the goals you've set for

yourself have happened or are happening.
Tick off goals you've accomplished (and pat yourself on the back)

- Tweak any timelines on goals if you have to

- Bring in new goals (continue with the momentum!

- Adjust personal goals based on business goals (you might be doing better than you think – can you bring certain personal goals closer? E.g. Is it possible to allocate extra money to the mortgage to pay it down even quicker? Have you decided you want to prioritise a family holiday as a reward for hitting key metrics in your business)

- Adjust business goals based on personal goals (you might now be focusing on putting extra money aside for an investment property, so now you need to come up with new business goals to ensure you're able to do this)

- Personal and business goals are quite linked in that you're always wanting to make sure your BUSINESS goals are letting you hit your PERSONAL goals. So, when conducting your monthly review, you want to analyse the progress of both and tweak accordingly. The world's your oyster, so make sure you keep pulling from W.I.S.H List and turning those Big Dreams into goals!

- If you don't already have a business coach, you can book in for a free 90-minute strategy session here: www.actioncoachgeelong.com.au

Big Ticket Budget

WHAT To Review:

You want to check in with your Big Ticket Budget – that is, your financial plan for how you're going to afford your goals! Are you spending more or less than you'd planned? If so, tweak accordingly. If you've added in new goals, make monetary adjustments to so you can afford to make these happen!

WHEN to review:

Review every 6 months.

HOW To Review:

Look at your current Big Ticket Budget and see if your numbers still "stack up." Run through the steps again, making tweaks when needed. (For example, do you need to give yourself more or less to spend on Base Living Costs like groceries and electricity? Or are you now planning to put money aside to save up for the boat purchase in a couple of years? Add that cost in.) Realistically, Step 3 is likely the place that will need your attention the most during this review stage.

Here are the steps for the review process:

1. Step 1: Adjust Your "Base Living" Costs If Needed
2. Step 2: Adjust Any Costs To Achieve Your Big Ticket Assets (often this is unnecessary as it's already been factored in over the long term)
3. Step 3: Add In The Costs To Achieve Your Other Yearly Goals

Business Progress

WHAT To Review:

Check in with how your business is progressing regularly! Review:

- Business Goals (for a quick progress report, this happens weekly in team meetings – your big ones happen monthly)
- Business Foundations – Time & Financials especially!
- Business Strategy (fortnightly)
- Profit & Loss Statement (monthly)
- Team Performance (at least 6 monthly)

WHEN to review:

Ideally, you want to be reviewing your Business every 2 weeks with a qualified business coach.

HOW To Review:

Speak directly with your business coach so you are regularly measuring, managing and tweaking the vital areas of your business! If you are not in a position to speak with a business coach use the materials in this book to support you as you undertake your review process. I also run what's called 'The Wealthy Tradie Workshop' (this is outside my normal business coaching) that will walk you through this entire process and help you with any tweaks and adjustments.

Please note: this is a paid live event and only a limited number of tradie owners can attend a workshop, so if you're interested in attending, please reach out to me ASAP. (If you're a client, you get free access as part of my coaching service.)

Book your FREE strategy session here:
https://actioncoachgeelong.com.au/
Give me a quick call today: 0409 402 474

Conclusion

While you're at the 'end of the road' in terms of this book, I hope what has begun is just the beginning of a very exciting and rewarding journey for you.

The fact is most tradie owners will continue to work just to keep their heads above water, getting swallowed up in the day-to-day, and busting their guts just to stay afloat. They will never really know that there is another way to run their business that doesn't involve working all the time, feeling stressed and overwhelmed at almost every moment and wondering if they really would be 'better off' working for someone else.

But you have changed that for yourself. You now know that becoming a Wealthy Tradie – one who is financially rich, time rich, energy rich and has great relationships – is not just something 'other people' can achieve. It's totally possible for you. You now have the system; all you need to do is simply use it… and you'll be set for life!

The reality is unless you are taking action on what's inside this book, nothing will change for you. Reading a book never made anyone wealthy – ACTING on what's inside the book will.

You must first define what wealth is for you (whether it's taking regular family holidays, saving to buy or pay off a house, or making sure you have enough to retire early), and then making the necessary changes in your business to make sure this stuff actually happens! It's not rocket science, but it does require you to DO something about it. If you keep waiting until you 'have the time' to make change, what you are effectively saying to yourself is this: I do not prioritise my life. Remember: your business is not your baby... your life is far more important!
Don't wait until something really bad happens to FORCE you into taking this stuff seriously. This is coming from someone who had to lose almost everything to understand.

From the outset, this book has been about managing money... but what it's really about at its core is making sure you achieve your dreams while you're here. Only after we ask ourselves "What are the dreams you'd like to fulfil?" do we look at how much money is required to make that a reality. Then we get our business to deliver that amount for you, so you can get on with the joy of living!

My life is considerably more fulfilled since I began using this system. I am now able to spend quality time with my five boys – we go hiking and camping, and kick the footy whenever we can. I've finally taken the motorbike trips I'd been dreaming about, and the fishing trip to Kakadu in the stinking heat (caught heaps of fish… and mosquito bites!), and have already carved out the time in the calendar for my sailing trip in Croatia and the rest of it!

But best of all, I have peace of mind now – that financial security that wasn't there even just a few short years ago is there now – and that's honestly priceless. I know I'm chipping away at my own superannuation and investment goals, and I'll be able to take care of myself and my family when I retire. I'm also laser-focused on what I need to do in my own business to keep chipping away at these goals too. So, I'm not just some guy harping on about this stuff – I'm living it, and I'm living proof that it works.

I also have the opportunity to guide my clients through this system so that they can achieve the same results and feeling for themselves, which is just amazing. I take regular workshops that literally walk these tradies through the system, so they've got someone not just to teach them how it all works in a way that's easy to understand, but also hold them accountable to their own goals so their dreams actually come true.

It's been brilliant to see how keen they then become to make those necessary changes in their business, and how quickly the results come in with steady, purposeful progress. I'm currently working on getting one of my clients into his first house, which is a feeling that's a bit hard to describe.

Like I said, from the outset it seems like it's just about money, but it's not... it's about taking those dreams and turning them into a reality. Your trades business becomes the vehicle, not the ultimate destination. I've also got guys who've split their 'on the tools' time in half, have started their own share portfolios and taken action so they can take a much-needed break from their business without feeling guilty or stressed out about it.

The Wealthy Tradie is not just a proven system – it's a new way of doing business that will completely transform your relationship with your business, your team, your family and even yourself... because once you're on track to REAL wealth, everything changes in the best way possible. I guess you approach life differently... and well, life rewards you for that. I wish you all the best on your own journey to wealth – it's a ripper!

Your Next Steps

Congratulations on getting this far and hopefully knocking off at least some of the hardest work you can do.... working on yourself! Having created your big-ticket budget is light years ahead of the average business owner. The next big steps are how to turn your business into your wealth generator and make your business work for you.

This is exactly how we help business owners through the coaching practice. We help them identify:

- The proven strategies and "business hacks" to get their time back.

- How to control cashflow and navigate the finance stuff so their business funds their personal wealth both today and in retirement.

- What action to take (and prioritize) in their trades business starting now.

Imagine if your business paid for your dream lifestyle, literally all of it. Not just for today, but even when you put down the tools for good and retire.
Imagine NOT being flat out or on the go all the time, and instead being level-headed, clear and respected because you know you've got all of the time, money and resources behind you to take confident action in your business that benefits everyone.

And finally, imagine customers literally knocking on your door and leaving rave reviews about what it was like to work with your company, celebrating with a team who loves working for you, and coming home to a family who feels taken care of and grateful to have you in their life.
How good would that feel?

See, the thing is, this is entirely possible for you and every tradie owner out there. We've just been fed a lie that we need to bust our guts to get work, keep work, and earn a decent living, but this is a myth. Working around the clock leads to exhaustion and frustration, not real wealth. And real wealth is not just about the dollars. Sure, money absolutely plays a role, but real wealth is also about having time, energy, optimal health and great relationships.

Be honest: As it currently stands, is your business currently generating REAL wealth for you? If not, we need to make some changes beginning right now.

Let's get one thing clear: Performing a trade and owning a business is not the same thing! As the owner you are exactly that - the owner, not the operator. So, you need to park the hands-on trades stuff for a moment and focus on business because here's the trick - your business is your key to real wealth.

Unlike an employee who MUST hand over their time and effort in order to get paid, a business owner is in a magnificent position where we don't have to do this if we know how to run our business correctly and effectively. We pay someone else to do the labor, which gives us our time and energy back, and provided we're earning a profit in the process which we should ALWAYS be, we get paid for someone doing the hard work for us.

Best of all, when we play our cards right, we can purposely design the business to spit out enough cash for us to live our dream lifestyle. And because nobody's dream lifestyle involves being sick, broke, exhausted, criticized or lonely, this means you'll hit a home run to real wealth! Very nice indeed.

So, what do we need to do in your business to turn it into your wealth generator instead of your pain in the arse? If you want help with that right now, let's start a conversation.

Work With Me

If you're sick of working all the time and aren't sure where all the money is for all your hard work, or if you know there's a gap in your skills and you need help building wealth through your trades business, I can help in one of three ways:

1. Private One-On-One Coaching

Here we sit down together and work one-on-one to build your business and get it generating the wealth you're after. Because every business (and indeed every business owner) is different, this is tailored business coaching to suit your unique needs, goals and aspirations. As a licensed ActionCOACH Business Coach, I am experienced in, and able to assist you with, the strategic design and implementation of activities such as time management, systems, recruitment, teambuilding, financial reporting, sales and marketing, owner motivation and more.

The first step in this process is a free strategy session where I get to know you and your business and walk you through the coaching process to determine how I can best serve you and your business during our one-on-one time together. I like to get my clients results so my coaching process comes with a guarantee. I meet all my clients face-to-face to make sure we're on the same page when it comes to maximizing the performance of their business.

I have an office in Geelong where you can literally walk in and have a chat with me and I only work with tradies, so I understand your business unlike some other coaches who sit in suits all day! I've been in the business for over a decade and I'm ready and willing to get you results.

If you're keen to build your wealth and get tangible results in your business starting today, please head to www.actioncoachgeelong.com.au or call me directly on 0409 402 474 for a free no-obligation coaching session.

2. The Wealthy Tradie Workshop

This is full-day live event where I walk you through The Wealthy Tradie system in its entirety and we cover all the critical activities to build wealth through your business together. You will have the opportunity to ask me any questions you have and will walk away with a personalized business and wealth plan that you can put into place immediately. This workshop is unique to tradie business owners and will give you the mindset to uncover your personal dreams and goals, as well as the proven process to get your business delivering them!

The aim of the workshop is to tie all of these together and make sure you retire wealthy and happy, while having a great time along the way. This is a live event that I run only at specific times throughout the year, so spaces are limited and you must get in quick to secure your spot. If you are a current client of mine, this event is completely free to you. If you would like to find out more about this live workshop please visit:

www.wealthytradie.com.au/workshop
or call me directly on **Ph: 0409 402 474.**

3. Group Coaching

This is suited to tradie owners who are just starting out or who are running a one-man business. While you're still spending a serious chunk of your time on the tools, you see a huge opportunity to grow and improve the way you operate. For this reason, you've recognized the need for a coach, but for cashflow and time reasons, you're happy to learn the business fundamentals alongside two or three other business owners in a similar position.

You will need to be a self-starter and recognize that the work we achieve together in a group setting will never be as tailored as one-on-one coaching; however, you will absolutely get benefit from this level of coaching as well as the unique opportunity to learn from other tradie owners in a similar position as you. If you're keen to find out more about group coaching, please visit:

www.actioncoachgeelong.com.au

If you're finding yourself working all the time, or are stressed and overwhelmed in your trades business, it's time to pivot to the easier and smarter way of doing things. Invest in yourself and start seeing results today. This is a proven system to follow and you don't need to go it alone or struggle when you simply don't have to mate!

I want to encourage you to contact me or my team. There is a better way to do business and I know I can help.

Let's get you building wealth through your trades business!

To your success,

Hugh Bowman
hugh@actioncoachgeelong.com.au
www.actioncoachgeelong.com.au
Ph: 0409 402 474